THE YUMMY
CHAR GRILLER

GRILL & SMOKER

COOKBOOK

1000-DAY YUMMY AND FAMILY-APPROVED RECIPES FOR ANYONE WHO WANT TO ENJOY TASTY EFFORTLESS DISH

CATHY CABAN

CONTENTS

INTRODUCTION

What Wood Pellet Grills Are

A wood pellet grill is basically a hybrid between a smoker, a traditional grill, and an oven. They can be used for many different types of cooking, even searing and baking. Wood pellets are used for fuel. Some wood pellets are meant to last a long time, while others focus on enhancing flavor.

Pellet grills do not cook food over a direct flame. Instead, they heat food indirectly by circulating the warmth through the grill, much like what an oven does.

How the Char Griller Wood Pellet Grill Works

A pellet grill looks like a gas grill, with a metal hopper mounted to one side to house the wood pellets they burn as fuel. The resulting fire imparts a smoky taste because the wood pellets are made from flavorful hardwood species such as hickory, oak, pecan, and cherry.

Today's pellet grills feature an electronic thermostat with a digital display, so you can dial in a precise cooking temperature; the hopper automatically draws the appropriate amount of pellets into the firebox, where they're ignited. The grill holds the temperature steady, like an oven, adjusting the rate at which it burns pellets to maintain that set temperature.

The Benefits You'll Gain from Your Char Griller Wood Pellet Grill

There are some key advantages to be enjoyed when using a pellet smoker. We've covered the most important below.

1. A pellet smoker offers more options and versatility than a standard smoker. Depending on the model you choose, it will be possible to roast, smoke, barbecue, and even bake inside your pellet smoker.
2. Pellet smoking offers the best results for smoked meat. This is because they are designed specifically to infuse maximum smoke flavor with indirect heat. When compared to smoking in a normal grill, the results are far better. For rich and complex flavor, a dedicated pellet smoker is an ideal choice.
3. Flavor options are virtually unlimited. Pellet chips are made from natural wood pieces, with flavors like hickory, maple, apple, mesquite, cherry, and more.

4. Temperature management is simple because most pellet smokers have advanced designs with automatic timing and heat control. The hopper ensures a consistent level of smoke throughout cooking.
5. Most models reach smoking temperature within ten to fifteen minutes. Only gas grills are easier and faster to get to cooking temperature.
6. Pellet smokers are designed for serious home cooks, so they are generally large, offering plenty of cooking space. This means you can easily cook whole turkeys, chicken, duck and other game, large BBQ cuts, and anything else that you want to infuse with a rich flavor.
7. Unlike a charcoal or gas smoker, pellet models are easy to use. There's no need to measure or weigh the wood that you will use. Pellets are distributed as needed and cooking temperature is regulated by an electronic thermostat.
8. Value is incredible because a high-quality pellet smoker will last for many years without problems. Even though the initial price might be higher than a comparable gas or charcoal grill, longevity, ease of use, and amazing results add value.

Using Tips for Your Char Griller Wood Pellet Grill

1. Take advantage of your pellet grill's searing capabilities.

Many pellet grills feature searing capabilities, meaning they can reach temperatures over 500 degrees. Again, check your owner's manual for information on your specific model.

2. Use lower temperatures to generate more smoke.

You'll generate more smoke at lower temperatures, particularly in the "low and slow" range between 225 and 275.

3. Use the reverse sear method.

Don't be afraid to smoke your meat at a lower temperature, then finish it at a higher temperature. This two-step approach is especially useful for smoking chicken with crisp (not rubbery) skin, or the "reverse sear method" often employed for thicker steaks or prime rib

4. Never allow the pellets in the pellet hopper to run out.

Never allow the pellets in the pellet hopper to run out. If this happens, consult your owner's manual before relighting the grill. If you must, set a timer to remind yourself to top off the pellets.

5. Experiment with pellet flavors.

Experiment with pellet flavors. Some brands of pellets are fairly subtle.

Better to Clean Your Char Griller Wood Pellet Grill

It is often easiest to clean the inside of your grill at the same time as the outside because your grill will already be unplugged, cold and emptied of wood pellets. Cleaning the inside of your pellet smoker involves several steps to ensure proper pellet grill maintenance, including cleaning the grease drip tray, vacuuming and scraping the burn pot and scrubbing the grill grates.

1. GREASE DRIP TRAY

To clean the grease drip tray, first remove the grill grates and any extra cooking racks. Use a griddle scraper to scrub grease off of the surface of the tray and remove the scrubbed grease using a paper towel. Wipe the grease drip tray clean using a cloth or paper towel. If you want to clean your grease drip tray with soapy water or liquid cleaner, remove the tray from the BBQ first. Dry the tray completely before putting it back into your pellet smoker.

2. BURN POT

Regular pellet grill ash clean-out keeps your smoker operating in top condition. A clean smoker provides even cooking and produce the best tasting pulled pork, ribs, and grilled veggies — or anything else you want to cook.

To clean your burn pot, first remove the grease drip tray and heat deflector to access the burn pot. Pay attention to how they are installed so you can put them back in when you are done. The burn pot will often have a lot of ash build-up and debris that you will need to remove. The simplest way to clean your pellet smoker's burn pot is with a vacuum cleaner or ash vac. Use the hose to suck out all the ash and then wipe away any remaining ash or soot using a clean rag.

When deep cleaning your pellet grill after winter, you can take this a few steps further and scrub the interior walls of the smoker to remove any accumulated grease or dirt. After vacuuming the ash, use a scraper with a flat edge to dislodge scale from the sides of the smoker chamber. Scrub the loosened dirt with a non-metallic brush and wipe the fire pot with a clean cloth.

You can use a damp cloth to wipe the interior of the grill, but never put water directly into the burn pot. Use caution not to damage the electric elements and allow the grill to dry completely before use. Once your burn pot is clean, replace the heat deflector, drip tray, and grates.

If your grill is equipped with an ash container, now is a great time to empty it. Ash collection systems make it easy to remove ash build-up and allow you to clean your burn pot less often, as they collect much of the ash that normally builds up inside your pellet smoker.

3. GRILL GRATES

Cleaning your pellet smoker grates every time you use your grill keeps your food tasting delicious and fresh so your cookout guests are always satisfied. There are two ways to clean your grill grates; cold or hot. Follow these steps for how to clean your grill before or after use:

Cold Method (Before Cooking):

Ensure your grill is unplugged and cool:

Remove grates from grill and clean with bbq degreaser or soap and water. Some pellet grills may have dishwasher safe grates. If not, they can be cleaned in a sink or with a pressure washer or garden hose. If they are painted, be careful with using a pressure washer.

Scrub the grates thoroughly: Use a brush or spatula to scrub the grates to remove any residue that remains.

Hot Method (After Cooking):

Set your grill to the highest temperature: Grill grates are easiest to clean when they are hot — and your grill will do most of the work for you. After you cook, turn your grill to the highest temperature and allow it to heat up completely.

Do a burn off: Wait 10 to 15 minutes to let your grill burn away the remaining food and grease on the grill grates. Performing a burn off loosens any stuck-on grease and makes it easy to scrape off the ash.

Scrub the grates thoroughly: Use a brush or spatula to scrub the grates to remove any residue that remains. Because the grill will be hot, it is best to use a long-handled brush or scraper. You may also choose to clean your grill grates while wearing an oven mitt or grill glove to prevent burns.

POULTRY

Chicken Lollipops By Jeremy Souza

Ingredients:

- ➤ Chicken Drumsticks
- ➤ Favorite Seasoning
- ➤ Favorite Sauce or Glaze
- ➤ Charcoal
- ➤ Smoking Wood Chunks

Directions:

1. Transform the drumsticks into lollipops Using a sharp knife and kitchen shears cut around the chicken ankle to create the handle Remove the skin, meat, tendons, and cartilage to expose the bone. This will be your "lollipop stick" Remove any loose tendons with the kitchen shears To ensure that the chicken legs will stand up straight, flatten the bottoms with a sharp cleaver Cover the chicken leg handles with foil to protect from burning and discoloration Season the chicken liberally with your favorite seasoning. We decided to go with a habanero seasoning to pair with a sweet apricot glaze to come later Preheat your grill or smoker and set it up for 2 Zone Cooking (Direct and Add any smoking chunks or chips at this point if you wish Place the chicken on your grill away from the direct heat and allow to cook and smoke until an internal temperature of 165*F is reached At this point it's time to sauce! Use your favorite sauce and coat each drumstick Return to the smoker and cook for an additional 10 minutes Remove from the smoker and glaze one last time until they're nice and saucy Remove the foil, plate them nicely on a platter and enjoy. These are sure to impress!

Smoked Turkey Legs

Cooking Time: 3.5 Hrs

Ingredients:

- 1 Gallon of Water
- 1 cup of Kosher Salt
- 2 Tbsp of Garlic (Minced)
- 2 Tbsp of Ground Black Pepper
- 4 Tbsp of Garlic Powder
- 4 Tbsp of Onion Powder
- 1/3 Cup of Brown Sugar
- 2 Tbsp of Dried Basil
- 2 Tbsp of Dried Sage
- 2 Tbsp of Dried Thyme
- 1 Tsp of Paprika
- 1 Tsp of Cayenne Pepper
- 2-3 Bay Leaves

Directions:

1. Combine all the brine recipes in a large pot and bring to a boil. Let it cool. As it boils, rinse the turkey legs. Once the brine cools, submerge the turkey legs in it. Cover and refrigerate it overnight. Heat your smoker to 225-250°F. Remove the turkey legs from the refrigerator and pat dry with paper towels, allowing them to sit for 15-20 minutes. Transfer the turkey legs to the smoker and cook for 3-4 hours until the legs have a dark exterior and the juices run clear.

2. Allow them to rest for 10-15 minutes before serving as is, with barbecue sauce and with any desired sides

Grilled Chicken And Vegetable Kebabs

Cooking Time: 15 Min

Ingredients:

- 2 lbs. boneless, skinless chicken thighs
- 1 C. whole yogurt
- 2 Tbsp. unsalted butter, melted
- 1 Tbsp. salt
- ½ Tsp. ground coriander
- ¼ Tsp. ground turmeric
- Pinch red pepper flakes, optional
- 1 garlic clove, finely grated
- 3 bell peppers, stemmed and cored
- 1 red onion, cut into wedges
- 2 Tbsp. olive oil
- Flatbread, for serving
- Fresh mint and parsley leaves, chopped, for garnish
- Bamboo skewers

Directions:

1. Rinse chicken, pat dry with paper towel and cut into 2" thick pieces. Whisk together yogurt, butter, salt, coriander, turmeric, red pepper flakes and grated garlic in a medium bowl until smooth.

2. Add chicken and toss to evenly coat. Cover bowl with plastic wrap and let marinate at room temperature for 1 hour.

3. Rinse produce. Slice peppers into 2" thick pieces. Toss peppers and onion wedges in a medium bowl with the olive oil, and season with salt, to taste.

4. Soak bamboo skewers in water for 30 minutes. Divide chicken and vegetables evenly between the skewers, alternating between the two.

5. Pre-heat grill to 400°F. Grill kebabs, turning as needed, until the chicken has cooked through, about 15-20 minutes. Chicken is done when internal temperature reaches 165°F.

6. Let rest for 3-5 minutes, then garnish with chopped mint and parsley leaves, and serve with flatbread.

7. Enjoy!

Asian Chicken Salad

Cooking Time: 25 Min

Ingredients:

- 4 Cups Mixed Greens
- 2-3 Chicken Breasts
- 1/2 Cup Chopped Carrots
- 1/2 Cup Chopped Cucumber
- 1/2 Cup Chopped Radish
- 1/2 Cup Chopped Cilantro
- 1 Cup Cooked Quinoa
- 1/2 Cup Crispy Wonton Strips
- 1/2 Cup Soy Sauce (Marinade)
- 1/2 Cup Rice Wine Vinegar (Marinade)
- 1/4 Cup Sesame Oil
- 2 Tbsp Chili Garlic Paste or Sriracha
- 2 Tbsp Honey

Directions:

1. Whisk ingredients for marinade and reserve half.

2. Add 2-3 chicken breasts to the remaining marinade and let it sit for at least 30 mins.

3. While your chicken is marinating, preheat your Char-Griller to high heat, scraping your grates to keep your chicken from sticking! Grill chicken for 10-12 mins per side, until inside temp reaches 165. Let rest 10 mins before slicing.

4. Add chicken to a bed of mixed greens with an assortment of veggies the remaining veggies, and pro-tip: I always have a bag of crispy wonton strips in the pantry, so add those for a delicious crunch! Divide the dressing in half and store with the salad for a quick & easy week day lunch!"

Turkey Leg Lollipops

Cooking Time: 1.5 Hrs

Ingredients:

- 4 Large Turkey Legs
- 1/2 Cup Char-Griller Original Rub
- 1 Tbsp Olive Oil
- 3/4 Cup BBQ Sauce of Choice
- 1/4 Cup Apple Juice
- 1 tsp Honey
- 1 tsp Char-Griller Original Rub (For Sauce)

Directions:

1. With your boning knife cut where the turkey meat starts to thin out going towards the joint. Cut all around the bone and use a paper towel to help with the removal of the skin and joint. Tip: You will notice tendons and a little bone that runs parallel to the leg after you have cut it. Make sure to remove these with your boning knife or kitchen shears.

2. Wrap the exposed bones in foil (this will help with presentation).

3. Next, rub the turkey legs down with olive oil and apply seasoning liberally to lollipops. Make sure to get as even as a coat as possible.

4. Get your grill between 325 F and 350 F. Add hickory chunks to give the meat an extra layer of flavor.

5. Once the grill is up to temp put the turkey legs on indirect heat.

6. Start preparing the glaze by combining BBQ sauce, apple juice, honey, and seasoning in a microwavable safe cup. Set aside till it is time to glaze. Tip: Warm your sauce up right before it is time to glaze so that it is smooth and doesn't tack on the meat too heavily.

7. Once your turkey has reached internal temp around 165 F it is time to glaze. Dip each turkey lollipop into the cup with your glaze mixture until you have obtained a nice shine.

8. Quickly put the turkey back on the grill and let the internal temp reach 170 F.

9. Pull the turkey and let rest for 10 minutes before you eat. Enjoy!

Smoked Carolina Turkey

Ingredients:

- 10-12 lb. turkey
- 3 Tbsp. red pepper flakes
- ¼ C. paprika
- ¼ C. ground mustard
- ½ C. brown sugar
- 2 Tbsp. coarse black pepper
- 2 Tbsp. Kosher salt
- 2 Tbsp. melted butter

Directions:

1. Pour melted butter over turkey, or use marinade injector to inject butter into turkey
2. Mix red pepper flakes, paprika, ground mustard, brown sugar, black pepper and salt in small bowl to create seasoning mix
3. Rub turkey all over with seasoning mix
4. Place turkey on grill over indirect heat at 250°F or use Smokin' Stone
5. Inject turkey with its own juices every other hour
6. Cook time is 1 hour per pound or until turkey reaches internal temp of 165°F

Picnic "fried" Chicken

Cooking Time: 35 Min

Ingredients:

- 6 bone-in chicken thighs
- 3 Tbsp. Chicken BBQ rub
- 2 C. dried bread crumbs
- 2 eggs, beaten
- ½ C. buttermilk

Directions:

1. Rinse chicken thighs and pat dry with paper towel.

2. Prepare breading by mixing Chicken BBQ rub with bread crumbs in gallon sized storage bag.

3. Whisk eggs with buttermilk in large bowl until smooth. Dip chicken thighs in egg/buttermilk mixture and evenly coat all sides.

4. Place chicken thighs in bag with breading mixture, seal bag and shake gently to even coat thighs on all sides.

5. Place breaded chicken thighs on a cast iron griddle in the middle of the grill at 375°F for 35 minutes. Chicken thighs are done when internal temperature reaches 165°F.

Turkey Tips

Cooking Time: 3½ Hrs

Ingredients:

- 7-8 lb. turkey breast, cubed
- 1 medium onion, thinly sliced
- Chicken BBQ rub
- BBQ sauce
- 1-2 Tbsp. butter
- Salt and pepper, to taste

Directions:

1. Place turkey in a large roasting pan in an even layer, add BBQ sauce and turn to evenly coat. Allow to marinate for an hour.
2. Pre-heat grill to 230°F. Place pan with turkey on the grill and smoke for 30 minutes per pound or until internal temperature reaches 165°F.
3. While turkey is smoking, place a cast iron skillet on the grill and heat until very hot.
4. Remove turkey from roasting pan and add to skillet with onions, butter and more BBQ sauce. Allow to smoke for an additional 25 minutes, stirring occasionally.

Cherry Chipotle Buffalo Wings

Cooking Time: 1 Hrs

Ingredients:

- 4 lbs. chicken wings
- 14 oz. bottle cherry Chipotle BBQ sauce
- 3 Tsp. dried minced onion
- 2 Tsp. Chipotle chili powder
- 1 ½ Tsp. garlic powder
- 1 ½ Tsp. chili powder
- ½ Tsp. smoked paprika
- 2 C. sour cream
- 1 C. blue cheese salad dressing
- 1 C. blue cheese, crumbled
- 1 C. green onions, thinly sliced
- Salt and pepper, to taste

Directions:

1. Combine 1 Tsp rub, sour cream, salad dressing, crumbled blue cheese and green onions together in a medium bowl and mix well. 2. Refrigerate at least 2 hours to blend flavors.

2. Buffalo wings

3. Rinse chicken wings and dry with paper towel. 2. Combine dried minced onion, Chipotle chili powder, garlic powder, chili powder, smoked paprika and salt and pepper, to taste, into a small bowl and mix well. Reserve 1 Tsp. to mix with dipping sauce. Season chicken wings generously with rub. Place wings on the grill, equally spaced in rows, to smoke for 30 minutes when grill temperature reaches 250°F. 4. After letting wings smoke, increase grill temperature to 350°F and cook wings until internal temperature reaches 165°F. 5. Brush on sauce during the last 15 minutes, flipping once and coating evenly every 5 minutes.

Creole Latin Spiced Rotisserie Chicken

Ingredients:

- Whole Chicken (Any Size)
- Olive Oil
- Creole Seasoning To Taste
- Sazon To Taste
- Adobo To Taste
- Fresh Parsley Flakes or Fresh Cilantro Flakes
- Kitchen Twine
- 1 Onion (Sliced)
- Char-Griller Grills Super Pro & Rotisserie Kit

Directions:

1. Rinse and pat dry chicken. Trim access fat and skin. Apply coating of olive oil to all sides of the chicken. Add Sazon, Creole and adobo seasonings. Add twine and knot the legs and also the wings over the breast. Add chicken to rotisserie rod and lock in using the rotisserie forks. Then Sprinkle fresh parsley or cilantro flakes on to the chicken. Slice onion and place on to a hook. Heat grill with lump charcoal: When coking over an open fire I don't cook at specific temperature. I begin with an equivalent of a 1/2 chimney full of lump charcoal and monitor the fire by feel. I place the charcoal in the middle of the grill in the back. As the charcoal burns I add pieces as the cook goes along. Place rotisserie chicken in the grill along with the onions. Roast chicken until internal 165°. Remove chicken and onions from the grill. Allow to rest for 15 minutes. Slice and enjoy!

Easy Chicken And Cheese Quesadillas

Cooking Time: 10 Min

Ingredients:

- ➢ Pack Of Soft Tortillas
- ➢ 2 Lbs Chicken Tenderloin
- ➢ Your Choice of Cheese
- ➢ Your Choice Of Other Toppings

Directions:

1. Bring your griddle to high / medium-high heat, throw down some oil and cook up your chicken. Once they are cooked and chopped up, move them off to the side.

2. Throw down a little more oil because the griddle may be pretty dry by now, then a couple of tortillas to brown and soften up.

3. After flipping the tortillas once, add your toppings. Start with cheese all over the tortillas, then add your other toppings only on one half of the tortilla.

4. Fold the tortilla in half to create your quesadilla. Press firmly to activate the 'cheese glue'.

5. Flip once more to ensure everything is melty goodness inside.

6. Cut with a pizza cutter and serve with your choice of dips!

Garlic Parmesan Chicken Wings

Cooking Time: 45-60 Min

Ingredients:

- 4 lbs. Chicken Wings
- 16oz. bottle Italian dressing
- 1 C. shredded parmesan cheese
- 1/2 Tbsp. onion salt
- 1/2 Tbsp. black pepper
- 1 C. butter
- 1 Tbsp. oregano
- 2 Tbsp. garlic powder
- A pinch of rosemary

Directions:

1. Add charcoal to one side of grill for indirect grilling, or use Smokin' Stone and add flavored wood chips/chunks if desired
2. Let grill preheat to 275°F
3. Place wings on indirect heat side of grill
4. Smoke wings for 45-60 minutes, until internal temp reaches 170°F
5. While wings are smoking, make garlic Parmesan sauce by mixing Parmesan cheese, garlic powder, onion salt, black pepper, butter, oregano and rosemary
6. Remove wings from grill and toss in garlic Parmesan sauce

2-burner Flat Iron Seasoned Chicken Breasts

Cooking Time: 20 Min

Ingredients:

- 4 Boneless Chicken Breasts
- 1/4 Cup of Extra Virgin Olive Oil
- 1 Lemon
- 1 Tbsp of Garlic Powder
- 1 Tbsp of Onion Powder
- 1 Tbsp of Italian Seasoning or choice of herbs
- 1 Tbsp of Char-Griller Lemon Pepper Rub
- 1 Tsp of Cayenne Pepper

Directions:

1. If you prefer to rinse your chicken breasts, do so in cold water. Pat completely dry with paper towels. In a resealable bag add olive oil, and all herbs and seasonings. Add chicken and seal the bag before mixing until all pieces are thoroughly coated. Place the bag(s) in the refrigerator for 1 hour-overnight. With Flat Iron preheated to medium heat, add chicken breast and generous squirt of water to the cooktop before covering with the Char-Griller Basting Dome. Keeping covered, allow it to cook for 9-10 minutes. Remove Basting Dome and generously squeeze juice from lemon over each chicken breast. Allow chicken to cook uncovered for 5-6 more minutes, letting water to evaporate and slight crusting to form on bottom before flipping once more. Cook chicken until the internal temperature reaches 165°F. Serve immediately. Enjoy!

Fried Chicken And Corn

Cooking Time: 10 Min

Ingredients:

- ➢ 2 C. flour
- ➢ 2 oz. corn starch
- ➢ 2 oz. paprika
- ➢ 1 Tbsp. cinnamon
- ➢ Salt & pepper to taste
- ➢ 4 ears of corn
- ➢ 4 oz. melted unsalted butter
- ➢ 1 Tbsp. paprika

Directions:

1. Soak chicken up to 24 hours in buttermilk and hot sauce
2. In a bowl mix corn starch, salt & pepper, cinnamon, and paprika
3. Mix ingredients well
4. Add chicken to mixture and coat thoroughly
5. Once coated, let sit for 30 minutes
6. Heat grill to 375°F
7. In a hot cast iron skillet, add chicken and oil
8. Cook chicken 3-5 minutes per side
9. Soak corn in saltwater for up to 24 hours
10. Boil them in butter water for 10 minutes before adding to grill
11. On a plate, mix paprika, salt, pepper, and melted butter
12. Mix and roll corn and cover with mixture
13. Add to grill and cook for 3-5 minutes

Creole Latin Spatchcock Turkey

Cooking Time: 1-2 Hrs

Ingredients:

- Whole turkey
- Kitchen Scissors & Pairing Knife
- Char-Griller Marinade Injector
- Creole Seasoning: Generous Coating
- Sazón Seasoning: Generous Coating
- Adobo Seasoning
- Garlic Powder
- Onion Powder
- Creole Butter Injectable Marinade (17 Oz)
- Fresh or Dry Cilantro
- Olive Oil
- Turkey Oven Bags
- Bucket Or Cooler
- Char-Griller Grill

Directions:

1. Chop up fresh cilantro and set aside.

2. Remove turkey from bag & remove everything inside the cavity area along with the plastic tie holding the legs. 3.Using kitchen scissors & pairing knife remove the backbone to Spatchcock the turkey. Also trim and remove any access fat & skin.

3. Flip Turkey breast side up & push down on the breast using both hands to help flatten the turkey.

4. Inject turkey with Creole Butter. Use any extra Creole & rub on breast under skin.

5. Generously add olive to the both sides of the turkey.Tip: continue to trim access fat & skin as you go along.

6. Generously season the turkey with Adobo, Sazón, Creole, onion powder & garlic powder. Then sprinkle cilantro 8. Place turkey in turkey/oven bag & place in bucket or cooler. Place in refrigerator & allow the turkey to rest for 12-24 hours. Cooking Directions 1. Remove turkey from bucket/cooler & allow to rest at room temperature for 1-2 hours. 2. Preheat your Char-griller Smoker to 240°. 3. Place turkey in smoker and smoke until the turkey reaches 165° internal temperature. Product tip: use the Char-griller remote thermometer or folding prob thermometer. 4. Check on turkey about every hour & baste turkey with butter & spritz with apple juice. Tip: rotate turkey in different directions to allow even cooking. 5. After turkey reaches 165° internal temperature allow the turkey to rest for a minimum of 25 minutes. Sprinkle additional cilantro. 7. Slice, serve & enjoy.

Barbecued Turkey

Cooking Time: 4 Hrs

Ingredients:

- 13 lb. turkey, cut into pieces
- 1/2 C. Chicken BBQ rub
- BBQ sauce for brushing

Directions:

1. Season both sides of turkey pieces generously with Chicken BBQ rub, or your favorite rub.

2. Smoke turkey pieces on the grill on direct heat at 225°F for 3 hours and then raise the temperature to 350°F for another hour to finish it off.

3. Brush one side of turkey pieces with BBQ sauce at the 30-minute mark.

4. Flip and brush the other side after 15 minutes. Remove turkey pieces when internal temperature reaches 165°F.

5. Note: The turkey's internal temperature will continue to increase by 5-10 degrees after you pull it off the grill.

Creole Hush Puppy Fried Chicken Legs & Thighs

Ingredients:

- 4 Chicken Legs & 4 Thighs
- 2 Cups of Milk
- Garlic Parsley Butter
- CharGriller Creole Seasoning
- Caribeque Lemon Garlic Seasoning
- 2 Tbs of Sazon
- Garlic Powder To Taste
- Black Pepper To Taste
- Crispy Creole Tony Chachere's Hush Puppy 9.5 Oz
- 1 Cup of All Purpose Flour
- 1/2 Cup of Panko Bread Crumbs
- Cayenne Pepper To Taste
- Lard For Frying
- Char-Griller Grills Hybrid Gas and Charcoal Grill With a Side Burner

Directions:

1. Garlic Parsley Buttermilk Prepping

2. In a large bowl add 2 cups Milk Add melted Garlic Parsley Butter: 4 oz. to the milk. -Full Garlic Parsley Recipe links: Written Recipe & Video Recipe Add Char-Griller Grills Lemon Pepper: to taste Add Caribeque Lemon Garlic: to taste Add Black Pepper to Taste Add Garlic powder to Taste Add Creole Seasoning to Taste Mix ingredients thoroughly. Rinse and clean the chicken legs and thighs with cold water and pat dry with a paper towel. Trim any fat or cartilage from the chicken. Place the chicken in the Garlic Parsley Butter Mixture and mix thoroughly. Place in the fridge for 6-24 hours.

3. Batter/Breading Prep

4. In a large pan add the hush puppy mix: 9.5 oz., All Purpose Flour: one cup and Panko Bread Crumbs: ½ cup Add Cayenne Pepper: to taste Add Creole Seasoning: to taste Add Sazon: 2 tbs Add Black Pepper: to taste Mix all the ingredients thoroughly. Remove the chicken from the fridge and bowl. Then place the chicken legs and thighs in the batter/breading. Tip: apply pressure onto the chicken so the batter/breading can be thickly applied to the chicken. Set aside while the cast iron skillet heats up.

5. Cooking Directions

6. Fire up your Char-Griller Grills Hybrid Gas and Charcoal Grill side burner using a large cast iron skillet with lard. Preheat the Cast Iron Skillet with the oil to 335°. Place the chicken into the cast iron skillet for 15 minutes or until internal temperature 175°. Tip: place the chicken thighs skin side down when placing into the cast iron skillet. Remove the chicken from the cast iron skillet and allow it to drain/cool for 7 minutes. Serve and Enjoy

PIZZA

Flat-iron Pizza Quesadillas

Cooking Time: 10 Min

Ingredients:

- ➤ 8 Flour Tortillas
- ➤ 1 Pack Of Pepperoni And Or Salami
- ➤ 2 Cups Of Mozzarella Cheese
- ➤ 4 Tbsp Of Butter Or Margarine
- ➤ 2 Cups Of Spaghetti Sauce
- ➤ 4 Tbsp Of Dried Basil And Or Oregano

Directions:

1. Heat Flat Iron to medium heat. Add butter to flat top and spread across allowing it to melt. Once heated, place 4 tortillas flat on top. Immediately layer cheese, oregano/basil, meat and more cheese on the tortilla. Top with another tortilla. (Optionally, you can make each tortilla its own mini-quesadilla by only layering meat and cheese on one half then folding it in half.) Allow the cheese to fully melt on the inside before using a spatula to flip each over, adding more butter to the flat top, if necessary. Once cheese is melted and tortillas are browned and crisped to your liking, remove from Flat Iron. Serve each quesadilla with spaghetti sauce for dipping. Enjoy!

Gravity 980 Grilled Pizza

Cooking Time: 12 Min

Ingredients:

- 1 Lb. Fresh Pizza Dough
- 1/4 Cup of Extra Virgin Olive Oil
- All Purpose White Flour
- 1 Cup of Fresh Mozzarella Cheese
- Optional Toppings: Pepperoni, Vegetables, Sausage, Bacon, etc.

Directions:

1. Remove the fire shutter from your Gravity 980, load and light the hopper, then preheat to 500-600°F. Add flour to your counter or cutting board before prepping your dough into the desired pizza shape. Add pizza sauce, olive oil and cheese then add your pizza to the pizza stone. Add any toppings that must be cooked then add to the grill. Cook the pizza for 8-12 minutes or until desired brownness. Add any remaining fresh toppings and serve immediately. Enjoy!

Meat Lovers Pizza

Cooking Time: 9 To 12 Min

Ingredients:

- Pre-made Pizza Dough
- Pizza Sauce
- Garlic Powder - 2 tsp
- Shredded Mozzarella - 1 to 1.5 Cups
- 8 to 10 Slices of Pepperoni
- 1-2 Slices of Ham - Chopped
- 1/2 Cup Spicy Sausage - Browned
- 1/2 Cup Ground Beef - Browned
- Parmesan Cheese - Grated
- 1/2 Cup Arugula
- Olive Oil - 1 Tbs
- Salt and Pepper to Taste

Directions:

1. This Meat Lover's pizza packs on the flavor with ham, spicy sausage, ground beef, pepperoni, and two types of cheese. The optional arugula can take it over the top with its peppery bite. Cook this hot and fast on the AKORN for restaurant quality crust.

2. Allow pizza dough to come up to room temperature (about 8 hours). Tip: Place Pizza Dough in a large plastic bag that seals for the best results.

3. Brown ground beef and spicy sausage. Set aside.

4. Preheat AKORN to 500-600 degrees Fahrenheit. Insert Smokin' Stone. Place Pizza Stone on grates to heat.

5. Shape dough into pizza on a cutting board covered in semolina.

6. Add desired amount of pizza sauce and garlic powder.

7. Add ground beef and sausage to pizza. Add pepperoni and ham. Add mozzarella cheese.

8. Add parmesan cheese to taste.

9. Place pizza on pizza stone. Close lid and cook for 9 minutes or until crust is crisp and cheese melted.

10. Remove from pizza stone and allow to rest for 5 minutes.

11. Toss arugula with olive oil, salt and pepper.

12. Top pizza with arugula if desired.

Grilled Caprese Pizza

Cooking Time: 6 To 8 Min

Ingredients:

- 1 Ball of Pizza Dough, Rolled out Thinly
- 1/2 Cup Pesto
- 1 Small Ball Fresh Mozzarella, Torn to Shreds
- 1/2 Cup Cherry Tomatoes, Halved
- 4-5 Fresh Basil Leaves, Whole or Torn
- 1 Tbsp Fresh Parsley, Chopped
- 1 Tbsp Fresh Parmesan, Shredded or Grated
- 2 Tbsp Olive Oil
- Salt & Pepper to Taste

Directions:

1. Preheat Char-Griller to high heat. Scrape and oil your grates well so the dough does not stick.
2. Spread 1 T of oil to one side of the dough, and place oiled side down on heat first. Immediately turn burners to low and let dough cook for 2-3 minutes that side, until dough bubbles up.
3. Brush remaining oil on uncooked side, and then carefully use spatula to flip dough over. Turn heat off.
4. Spread the dough evenly with pesto, and scatter the torn mozzarella and halved tomatoes over the top. Close the lid, and allow residual heat from the grill to finish cooking the pizza for 5 minutes.
5. Remove pizza from heat and add fresh basil, parsley, and grated parmesan. Serve while warm. Enjoy!

Fire-grilled Pizza

Cooking Time: 10-15 Min

Ingredients:

- 3 C. bread flour
- 2 Tsp. salt
- 3 Tbsp. vegetable oil
- 1 Tsp. sugar
- 1 packet rapid-rising yeast
- 1 C. water
- Corn meal, for dusting
- Tomato sauce
- Garlic powder
- Cheese, if desired
- Toppings of choice

Directions:

1. In a stand mixer fitted with a dough hook, add water and yeast to the bowl and mix well. Then add sugar, salt and vegetable oil and mix.

2. Add bread flour, 1 C. at a time, and mix until a dough forms. Add water as needed to keep dough from sticking to the sides of the bowl. 3. Remove dough and knead for 1 minute by hand, forming it into a ball. Lightly spray a bowl with cooking spray, add dough ball and lightly spray the top. Cover with plastic wrap and allow dough to rise for 1 hour, until doubled in size.

3. Note: Dough is enough to make 2 medium pizzas. Cut dough in half, wrap unused portion and refrigerate or freeze for later use.

4. Pizza

5. Lightly flour counter. Stretch and work dough by hand, kneading until a 12" circle forms. Transfer dough to a wooden pizza peel lightly dusted with corn meal, to prevent sticking. 2. Pre-heat grill to 450°F. Sprinkle pizza dough with garlic powder. Spoon a layer of tomato sauce in the center and spread around to edges of dough. 3. Sprinkle a layer of cheese on top, if desired. Place other toppings on top of cheese layer. 4. Place pizza on pizza stone and allow pizza to cook for 10-15 minutes with lid closed. Rotate pizza after 5 minutes to ensure even cooking. Remove pizza from grill and allow to rest for 4-5 minutes. Slice and enjoy!

Breakfast Pizza

Cooking Time: 10 To 12 Min

Ingredients:

- Pre-made Pizza Dough
- Sun-dried Tomatoes - 1 Cup
- 1 Fresh Mozzarella Ball
- Deli Ham - 4 slices
- 1 Egg
- 1 (8 oz) Jar Tomato Sauce
- Baby Spinach - 2 Cups
- Dried Basil to Taste
- Salt and Pepper to Taste
- Semolina
- Garlic Powder to Taste

Directions:

1. Allow pre-made pizza dough to sit at room temperature covered with a clean dishcloth for at least 6 hours.
2. Preheat grill to medium high heat
3. Add pizza stone to grill and allow to preheat
4. Spread out pre-made pizza dough on a cutting board covered with semolina
5. Cut up ham and spinach.
6. Cut mozzarella into thin slices
7. Add tomato sauce to pizza. (As much as desired.)
8. Season with Garlic Salt and Basil
9. Add mozzarella slices
10. Add ham, spinach, and sun-dried tomatoes.
11. Add extra semolina to pizza stone and carefully slide pizza on grill.
12. Tip: Have a friend help with this step.
13. Allow to cook for 7 minutes with the lid closed.
14. Open grill and crack one egg onto the pizza.
15. Close the lid and allow to cook for 3 to 4 more minutes or until egg white is opaque.
16. Remove from grill and let rest for 5 minutes.
17. Serve and enjoy

Pepperoni Pizza

Cooking Time: 3-5 Min

Ingredients:
- Pizza Dough/Crust
- Pizza Sauce
- Mozzarella Cheese
- Pepperonis
- Other Toppings

Directions:
1. Add a layer of sauce
2. Spread your favorite toppings
3. Add an even layer of cheese
4. Add more toppings if desired
5. Heat grill to 550°F
6. Place pizza on stone
7. Cook for 3-5 minutes
8. Slice and serve!

Grilled Fathead Pizza

Ingredients:

- 10 oz Shredded Mozzarella Cheese
- 1 Egg
- 5 oz Balanced Almond Flour
- 1 tsp Pizza Seasoning
- 1/3 Cup Marinara Sauce
- 1/2 Pound Ground Italian Sausage, Ground
- 15 Pepperoni Slices
- 1 Green Bell Pepper, Chopped
- 1/2 Red Onion, Chopped
- 1 can sliced black olives
- 1 can sliced mushrooms
- 1.5 Cups Shredded Mozzarella Cheese (Topping)

Directions:

1. Preheat grill to a low temp of about 250°.
2. Melt 10 oz mozzarella cheese in microwave in 30 second increments until all melted, add 1 egg & mix. Once egg is mixed add the almond flour, baking powder & pizza seasoning.
3. Knead with hands until well incorporated (for about 3 minutes).
4. Spread dough out on a baking sheet with parchment paper.
5. Put on grill for about 5-6 minutes until crust is turning golden.
6. Then take crust off the grill, flip over & put back on parchment paper.
7. Add toppings & then put back in the grill for about 10 minutes or until desired doneness.

Pesto Burrata Grilled Pizza

Cooking Time: 3 Min

Ingredients:

- 1 Pizza Dough Ball (Store bought Dough or Homemade Dough)
- 1 Cup pesto
- 1 Cup Fresh Greens (Arugula or Spinach)
- 2 Burrata Balls
- 1/2 Cup Fresh Basil Leaves
- 4 T Olive Oil
- Salt And Pepper To Taste

Directions:

1. Fill chimney with charcoal. Place over side burner and turn flame to high, allowing charcoal to catch fire. If you do not have the side burner on your Texas Trio, you can light paper under the chimney so that it catches. We are cooking on the Akorn Jr today, so prep the base for charcoal, scrape the grates to make sure they're clean, and grab your stone or cast iron for the pizza.

2. Once coals have heated through, about 20 minutes, add them to the base of the Akorn Jr and place grates over the coals, add cast iron, and close lid to allow grill to heat up.

3. Let's prep the pizza. Cut dough ball into four equal pieces and roll each piece out to a thin circle.

4. I like to plate up all my toppings and take them out to the grill so I can make the pizzas quickly. When it's time- add a drizzle of the olive oil to the stone or cast iron and lay the dough out. Flip after about 60 seconds, once the sides start to golden and you see some bubbles forming. On the now cooked side that is up- spread ¼ cup of the pesto, add half a ball of burrata and close the lid for an additional 1-2 minutes, until the pie is cooked through. Remove from heat and top with arugula, fresh basil leaves, a drizzle of olive oil, and salt and pepper. Repeat three more times until all the pies are done. Serve hot, and enjoy!

Flat Iron Cheesy Pizza Bagels

Cooking Time: 15 Min

Ingredients:

- 3 Bagels Cut in Halves (Whatever type you prefer)
- 1 Can of Pizza Sauce
- 1 Cup of Pepperoni or Salami (Sliced)
- 2 Cups of Mozzarella Cheese
- 2 Tbsp of Butter

Directions:

1. Melt 1 Tbsp of butter on Flat Iron over Medium Heat.

2. Place bagels face down in butter and allow 2-3 minutes for them to lightly toast. Remove from heat.

3. On a separate section of the griddle, warm pepperoni/salami over medium heat for 3-4 minutes then set aside

4. On a tray or large plate, assemble bagel pizzas by spreading each with sauce, then adding desired amount of pepperoni/salami and cheese on top.

5. Place each bagel pizza back on the griddle on another Tbsp of melted butter over on medium-low heat until cheese has thoroughly melted and the bottom is toasted. (It might help to cover each bagel pizza with a basting/grill cover)

6. Serve hot.

SEAFOOD

Cedar Plank Smoked Salmon

Cooking Time: 1-1.5 Hrs

Ingredients:

- Salmon fillets
- 1/3 C. olive oil
- 1/3 C. soy sauce
- 1/3 C. maple syrup
- ½ Tsp. cayenne pepper

Directions:

1. Rinse salmon and pat dry with paper towel. 2. Mix all ingredients together and pour evenly over salmon in an airtight container. Reserve some for basting and set aside. 3. Place in refrigerator and allow to marinate for 1 hour, or longer if desired. 4. Pre-heat grill to 275°F. Soak cedar planks in water for 3 minutes before placing on the grill to warm for 5-10 minutes. 5. Place salmon on cedar planks and smoke until the internal temperature of the fish reaches 145°F, basting with reserved marinade every 30 minutes.

2. Remove from grill and serve. Enjoy!

Rosemary Shrimp Skewers

Cooking Time: 5 Min

Ingredients:

- Shrimp Seasoned with Salt, Pepper, and Jerk Seasoning - 1 Pound
- Fresh Rosemary - Use full stalk and remove half of leaves to expose the stalk, this becomes your skewer

Directions:

1. Skewer two shrimp per skewer
2. Cook on grill at 350 degrees, 5 minutes per side till cooked thoroughly

Honey-bourbon Glazed Salmon

Cooking Time: 45-60 Min

Ingredients:

- 1 Cedar Plank
- 1 Wild Salmon Filet
- 1 Lemon, sliced
- Lemon pepper seasoning (to taste)
- ½ C. Bourbon
- Water (enough to cover the cedar plank)
- 3 Tbsp. Honey
- 1 oz. Bourbon
- 1 Tsp. Lemon Zest

Directions:

1. Remove the pin bones from the salmon filet with fish bone tweezers. Pour water and bourbon into a large baking dish and soak cedar plank for a minimum of 1 hour.

2. Place salmon filet on cedar plank, sprinkle with lemon pepper seasoning, to taste, and cover with sliced lemons.

3. Prepare the grill for offset smoking by adding citrus wood chunks to the Side Fire Box. Place the salmon on the grill and smoke at 250° - 275°F for approximately 45 - 60 minutes.

4. Mix the honey, bourbon and lemon zest together in a bowl to make the glaze. After 30 minutes, intermittently brush the honey/bourbon glaze on the salmon.

5. Enjoy the deliciousness!

2-burner Flat Iron Easy Shrimp Tacos

Cooking Time: 10 Min

Ingredients:

- 1 Lb. of medium-sized shrimp, deveined and peeled with tails removed
- 6-8 Flour or Corn Tortillas
- 1 Tbsp of Extra Virgin Olive Oil
- 1 Tbsp of Char-Griller Chili Lime or Taco & Fajita Rub
- 1/2 Tbsp of Garlic Powder
- 1/2 Tbsp of Onion Powder
- 1/2 Tbsp of Pepper
- A Dash of Salt
- Optional Toppings: Iceberg Lettuce, Sour Cream, Tomatoes, Cilantro, Salsa, Avocado

Directions:

1. Make these simple shrimp tacos as complex or as stuffed as you'd like. Our Rubs will take this dish to the next level, preparing it perfectly for whatever your taste buds have in mind.

2. Prep shrimp, by drying as much as possible with paper towels. In a bowl, combine shrimp with olive oil and all seasonings. With Flat Iron preheated to medium-high heat, add shrimp to cooktop and cook while occasionally stirring for about 5-6 minutes or until shrimp are no longer pink. Remove from Flat Iron. Add tortillas to the cooktop and warm up, cooking for 2-3 minutes per side. Assemble the tacos with desired toppings and serve immediately. Enjoy!

Fresh Garlic Parsley Butter Salmon

Cooking Time: 30 Min

Ingredients:

- ➢ Garlic Parsley Butter
- ➢ 2 (6 oz) Salmon Mignons
- ➢ Tajin to Taste
- ➢ Dry Parsley Flakes to Taste
- ➢ Olive Oil

Directions:

1. Make Garlic Parsley Butter
2. Add Tajin seasoning to butter to taste or use favorite seafood seasoning.
3. Add 1 tbsp. of Fresh Garlic Parsley to each salmon mignons patty.
4. Add dry parsley flakes to taste.
5. Preheat your Char-griller Premium Red Kettle 14822 to 350°.
6. Insert the Char-griller Chimney in the middle of the grill in the fire pit area and do not remove it and no need to release the coals.
7. The handle will not melt inside the Premium Kettles. This will give you a hot fire in the middle of the grill for easy cast iron cooking and also raises the charcoal. The middle small grill grate can be easily moved with a Char-griller grate lifter to add charcoal.
8. Add olive oil to your cast iron skillet: just enough to coat the bottom of the skillet and place over the fire to preheat.
9. Then place the salmon on the cast iron skillet.
10. Flip Salomon after 12 minutes and toss the melted fresh garlic parsley on all sides of the salmon using a spoon.
11. Add 2 additional tbsp. to the skillet for extra flavor.
12. Then move the cast iron skillet away from the middle of the grill for a quick offset cook for 15 minutes.Tip: Continuously add the melted fresh garlic parsley on all sides of the salmon using a spoon for extra flavor.
13. Enjoy!

Grilled Swordfish With Lemon-caper Sauce

Ingredients:

- 8oz. swordfish steaks
- 4 oz. jar capers, drained
- ½ C. mayonnaise
- ½ C. sour cream
- 1½ fresh lemons, juiced
- ½ Tsp. seasoned salt
- ¾ Tsp. white pepper
- 1 Tsp. dried minced onion
- 5 Tbsp. green onion tops, minced (optional, for garnish)

Directions:

1. Blend all ingredients, except green onion tops.
2. Transfer to bowl, cover with plastic wrap and refrigerate for 1 hour.
3. Swordfish
4. Season swordfish steaks on both sides with seasoned salt, to taste.
5. Place on the grill at 400°F for 10 minutes per side. Swordfish is ready when the internal temperature reaches 140°F.
6. Remove the fish and let it rest for 5-10 minutes before serving.
7. Sauce swordfish steaks with lemon-caper sauce and garnish with green onion tops.

Seared Scallops With Pancetta

Cooking Time: 15 Min

Ingredients:

- ➢ 12 U-10 Scallops
- ➢ 4 oz. pancetta, chopped
- ➢ ½ red onion or 1 shallot, minced
- ➢ 2 C. green peas, drained and divided
- ➢ 4 oz. Parmesan cheese
- ➢ 1 Tbsp. olive oil
- ➢ Juice of 1 lemon
- ➢ 4 oz. mint, divided
- ➢ Salt and pepper, to taste

Directions:

1. Pre-heat grill to 375°F. Fry pancetta in a cast iron pan for about 5 minutes and drain grease. Add minced red onion (or shallot, if substituting) and 1 C. peas to pan and season with salt and pepper, then add ½ of mint and stir to incorporate. Cook until warmed through. 2. Combine 1 C. peas and lemon juice, remaining mint, olive oil and Parmesan cheese in a food processor. Season to taste with salt and pepper and blend until smooth. 3. Rinse scallops and pat dry with paper towel. Season scallops with salt and pepper to taste on all sides. Place on the grill and sear for 3-5 minutes per side.

2. To serve, spoon peas onto plate, add scallops and top with pancetta mixture. Enjoy!

Lobster Roll

Cooking Time: 10 Min

Ingredients:

- ➢ 8 oz. lobster tails
- ➢ ½ C. mayonnaise
- ➢ 3 Tbsp. lemon juice
- ➢ 2 celery stalks, finely chopped
- ➢ 2 Tbsp. fresh parsley leaves, chopped
- ➢ 4 rolls, split and lightly toasted
- ➢ Melted butter, for brushing
- ➢ Salt and pepper, to taste

Directions:

1. Brush lobster with butter and place on the grill, shell-side up, at 400°F for 3-4 minutes. Flip and grill for another 5-6 minutes. Lobster is done when internal temperature reaches 135°F.

2. While lobster is grilling, stir together mayonnaise, lemon juice, celery, parsley in a large bowl and add salt and pepper, to taste.

3. When lobster has cooled, scoop meat from shells and roughly chop. Fold into mayonnaise mixture from Step

4. Butter both sides of rolls and fill with lobster mixture. Enjoy!

Creole Blackened Salmon

Cooking Time: 10 Min

Ingredients:

- 1 Salmon Filet
- Avocado Oil
- Char-Griller Creole Seasoning

Directions:

1. Preheat grill to 400F
2. Slice salmon filet into approx 3" portions.
3. Lightly coat portions in avocado oil and season using Creole seasoning.
4. Place salmon on grill (I like to use copper grill mats for fish) grill approx 5-6 minutes, flip salmon and grill another 3-4 minutes.
5. Remove and enjoy!!

Fish And Chips

Cooking Time: 12 Min

Ingredients:

- ➢ 4 cod filets
- ➢ 3-4 Idaho potatoes
- ➢ 1 C. flour
- ➢ 1 C. milk
- ➢ 1 egg
- ➢ 1 Tsp. Old Bay seasoning

Directions:

1. Heat grill to 350-400°F.
2. Let oil heat up in skillet until it sizzles when splashed with a few drops of water.
3. 3-4 Idaho potatoes with skin on, cut into french fries.
4. Let them soak in water for 20-30 minutes to remove excess starch.
5. Pat dry on paper towels before frying.
6. Fries are done when they begin to turn golden
7. Mix batter until only a few clumps of flour remain. Don't over mix.
8. Dredge fish in flour seasoned in Old Bay, if you prefer, before dipping in batter
9. Let fish filets fry on each side for 2-3 minutes, until golden crispy brown.
10. Serve with coleslaw and tartar sauce. Delicious!

Lobster Mac 'n Cheese

Cooking Time: 30-35 Min

Ingredients:

- 8oz. lobster tails
- 1 lb. Cavatappi or elbow macaroni
- 1 qt. milk
- 1 stick unsalted butter, divided
- ½ C. all-purpose flour
- 12 oz. Gruyere cheese, grated
- 8 oz. extra-sharp Cheddar, grated
- 1½ C. breadcrumbs
- ½ Tsp. black pepper
- ½ Tsp. nutmeg
- Kosher salt, to taste

Directions:

1. Butterfly the lobster. To do this, use a sharp knife or kitchen shears to split the lobster shell all the way to the tail. Slice the meat in half along the cut line on the shell, being careful not to slice through the lobster. Open the lobster shell-side down, lay it flat and brush with butter. 2. Place lobster on the grill, meat side down at 375°F for 4-5 minutes. Flip and grill for another 6-7 minutes. 3. While lobster is grilling, make the Mac 'n cheese. Lobster is done when internal temperature reaches 135°F. 4. Remove lobster from grill and allow to cool. Scoop meat from shells and roughly chop.

2. Mac 'n cheese

3. Pour oil into a large pot of boiling salted water. Add pasta and cook according to package directions, 6-8 minutes. Drain well. 2. Meanwhile, heat the milk in a small saucepan until hot, being careful not to boil it. Whisk together 6 Tbsp. butter and flour in a large pot. Add hot milk and cook for 1-2 minutes, until thickened and smooth. Remove from heat and add cheese, 1 Tbsp. salt, pepper, and nutmeg. Add cooked macaroni and lobster and stir well. Spoon mixture into cast iron pan. 4. Melt the remaining butter, stir in breadcrumbs and sprinkle on top. Place pan on the grill at 375°F and bake for 30- 35 minutes, or until the sauce is bubbly and the macaroni is lightly browned on top.

Grilled Chilean Sea Bass

Cooking Time: 30 Min

Ingredients:

- Whole Chilean Sea bass
- 2 oz. parsley, chopped
- 1½ oz. Original All-Purpose BBQ Rub or your favorite seafood seasoning
- 2 lemons, sliced
- 2-3 sprigs of dill
- Salt and pepper, to taste
- 4 oz. olive oil

Directions:

1. Pre-heat grill to 350°F. Place the charcoal on one side for indirect heat.
2. Score fish diagonally on each side in the thickest part of the meat.
3. Stuff the inside cavity with dill sprigs and lemon slices.
4. Season both sides of the outside of the fish to taste with olive oil, salt and pepper and top with an even layer of Original All-Purpose BBQ Rub, or use your favorite seafood seasoning, and parsley.
5. Lay the fish on the grill for 5-7 minutes on direct heat, then move to the indirect heat side for 15-20 minutes.

Blackened Catfish

Cooking Time: 15 Min

Ingredients:

- 4-6 Catfish Filets
- 3-4 Tbsp of Blackening Seasoning (Few Of My Favorites, Mis Rubins Fish Magic, Ashman Bayou Blackening, Pappys Lemon Pepper)
- 2 Tbsp Avocado Oil

Directions:

1. Preheat grill to 450F, I like to use a copper grill mat when grilling fish, works very well. Coat filets with oil and season. Place fish on grill mat, grill 6-8 minutes until you get desired blackened look, flip fish and cook another 3-4 minutes. Remove catfish from grill serve over rice and enjoy!

Grilled Tilapia

Cooking Time: 15-20 Min

Ingredients:

- ➢ 3 whole Tilapia
- ➢ 2 oz. smoked paprika
- ➢ 2 oz. Old Bay seasoning
- ➢ Salt and pepper, to taste
- ➢ Chopped parsley
- ➢ Olive oil
- ➢ 4 garlic cloves thinly sliced

Directions:

1. Set up grill for indirect heat and preheat to 350°F.

2. While grill is heating, stuff the inside of each fish with chopped parsley and garlic, then season inside and out with smoked paprika and Old Bay seasoning. Drizzle with olive oil and top with more parsley, smoked paprika/seasoning mix and remaining garlic.

3. Place fish on the grill oiled side down and drizzle with more oil and season with remaining parsley, smoked paprika/seasoning mix. Allow fish to cook for 7-10 minutes on each side.

4. Enjoy!

Cedar Plank Salmon

Cooking Time: 20-25 Min

Ingredients:

➢ Whole Coho Salmon 2 Lbs

➢ Cedar Plank Boards

➢ Olive Oil

➢ Kary's Roux All Purpose Seasoning

➢ Caribeque Lemon Garlic Seasoning

➢ Lemons

➢ Dill

➢ Parsley

➢ Asparagus (Optional)

➢ Garlic Parsley Butter

Directions:

1. Soak the cedar plank boards in water for one hour prior to prepping the salmon. Slice the whole salmon into four fillets, it is fine to leave the skin on. Place the salmon fillets on the cedar plank boards with a few lemon slices and asparagus. Tip: Apply olive oil directly on the cedar plank side you place the salmon to keep it from sticking.

2. Apply even coat of olive oil to the top/sides of the salmon fillets. Apply Caribeque Lemon Garlic Seasoning and Kary's Roux All Purpose Seasoning: use to taste. Add Garlic Parsley Butter to the top of each salmon: 1tsp per fillet. Add dill, parsley and additional lemons to the salmon fillets. Sprinkle parsley flakes when done to complete the prepping process.

3. Grilling directions: 20-25 minutes, internal temperature 145°

4. Preheat your grill to 400° Add cedar planks with the salmon to the grill directly over the lump Charcoal. No need to rotate, allow the grill, charcoal and cedar plank salmon to roast the salmon. Tip: It's also okay if your temperature drops: check out the recipe video on YouTube full for temperature control tips. Cook to internal temperature 145° and remove the cedar planks from the

5. Grill and it's ready for immediate eating. Tip: take the guesswork out and use the Char-Griller Grills folding probe to easily see what temperature the salon is at. Enjoy!

Steamed Mussels With Pancetta

Cooking Time: 30 Min

Ingredients:

- 2 lbs. fresh mussels, scrubbed and de-bearded
- 4 oz. pancetta, diced
- 3/4 C. dry white wine
- 2 Tbsp. olive oil
- 1/2 onion, diced
- 4 cloves garlic, peeled and minced
- 1 1/4 C. fish stock
- 2 Tbsp. lemon juice
- 2 Tbsp. chives, minced
- 8-10 grape tomatoes, sliced lengthwise
- Pinch of crushed red pepper flakes
- Salt and pepper to taste
- French bread, sliced and toasted for serving

Directions:

1. Add pancetta from Step 1 and mussels to pan and allow to steam with lid closed, until mussels have opened, about 5-10 minutes.

2. Open grill lid and stir in dry white wine, fish stock, lemon juice, chives, sliced tomatoes and crushed red pepper flakes, if desired, and season with salt and pepper, to taste. Simmer for 3-5 minutes until almost all of the liquid is evaporated.

3. Remove pan from the heat and discard any shells that do not open. Serve with toasted French bread. Enjoy!

Shrimp 'n Grits

Cooking Time: 20-25 Min

Ingredients:

- 1 lb. shrimp, peeled and deveined
- Original All-Purpose BBQ rub, to taste, or preferred rub
- ½ red bell pepper, chopped
- ½ onion, chopped
- Handful of cilantro, chopped
- 4 C. water
- 1 Tsp. salt
- 1 C. stone-ground grits
- 2-3 Tbsp. butter
- 4 oz. heavy cream
- 2 oz. Parmesan cheese
- Salt and pepper, to taste

Directions:

1. Pre-heat grill to 375°F. Bring water to a boil, add grits and cook until water is absorbed, about 20-25 minutes. Remove from heat, stir in butter, cheese and heavy cream. Add salt and pepper, to taste and stir. Set aside. 2. While grits are cooking, melt butter in skillet and sauté red pepper and onions until soft, about 5-7 minutes, stirring occasionally. 3. Add shrimp and season with Original All-Purpose BBQ Rub and cook for 3-5 minutes, until opaque and fully cooked. Add cilantro and salt and pepper, to taste and stir to combine.

2. To serve, spoon grits into bowls and top with shrimp and red pepper mixture. Garnish with more cilantro and enjoy!

BEEF

Reverse Seared Tri-tip Pico De Gallo

Cooking Time: 2 Hrs

Ingredients:

- Tri-Tip- 2 to 3 Pounds
- Kosher Salt- 1 Tablespoon
- Coarse Black Pepper- 1 Tablespoon
- Onion Powder- 1 Teaspoon
- Garlic Powder- 1 Teaspoon
- Hot Sauce- 2 Teaspoons
- Oak Splits
- Large Tomatoes (Chopped)- 2
- White Onion (Finely Chopped)- 1/2 Cup
- Cilantro (Finely Chopped)- 1/4 Cup
- Jalapeno (Seeds Removed to Preference, Finely Chopped)- 1/2 to 1 ounce
- Lime Juice- 2 Tablespoons

Directions:

1. Remove all excess fat and silver skin from the tri-tip. Mix together all the dry ingredients in a shaker until they are well blended. Use the hot sauce as a slather on both sides of the tri-tip to help get the rub to stick. Carefully season both sides and ensure that the tri-tip has a nice even coat of seasoning.

2. Start prepping your fire and working on getting your smoker up to 275 F. Once your smoker has reached 275 F it is time to put the tri-tip on and let the smoker do its job.

3. Once the tri-tip has reached an internal temperature of 125 F it is time to take it out of the smoker and prep for the sear. Place the tri-tip in a pan and cover with foil while you begin to get the grill up to 450-500 F.

4. Tip: you can get a good sear on either the grill or a cast iron skillet.

5. Once the grill has reached 450-500 F place the tri-tip directly on the grill and sear both sides till internal temp reaches 135 F. Pull the tri-tip off the grill and let rest for 15-20 minutes before slicing.

6. Tip: internal temp for beef varies by preference so feel free to pull it sooner for rare or later for well done.

7. Slice the tri-tip against the grain and top with Pico De Gallo. Enjoy!

8. Pico De Gallo Directions:

9. In a bowl combine the onion, jalapeno and lime juice. Salt to taste and let marinate for 3-5 minutes.

10. Add chopped tomatoes and cilantro into the bowl with the other ingredients. Stir well.

11. Let the mixture marinate so the flavors can meld. Serve and enjoy!

12. Tip: If you let the Pico De Gallo marinate for 1-3 hours the better the flavors will be when it is time to eat.

Italian-style Meatballs

Cooking Time: 10 Min

Ingredients:

- 1 lb. ground chuck
- ½ lb. ground pork
- ¾ C. breadcrumbs
- 2 eggs, lightly beaten
- 1/3 C. grated Parmesan
- 1/3 C. grated Pecorino Romano
- 2 cloves garlic, minced
- 2 Tbsp. finely chopped fresh parsley
- ¼ Tsp. red pepper flakes, optional
- Olive oil, for brushing
- Salt and pepper, to taste
- Marinara sauce, for serving
- Slider buns, for serving, optional

Directions:

1. Pre-heat grill to 400°F. Combine chuck, pork, breadcrumbs, eggs, Parmesan and Pecorino cheeses, garlic, parsley, and red pepper flakes in a large bowl and mix by hand until just blended. 2. Roll mixture into 1½" diameter meatballs. Season generously with salt and pepper, to taste. 3. Brush meatballs with olive oil and place on grill. Turn occasionally until well-browned on all sides and cooked through, 2-3 minutes per side. 4. Remove meatballs, serve with your favorite sauce and top with more cheese, if desired.

2. Alternately, transfer grilled meatballs and sauce to a pan on medium heat and turn to evenly coat. Serve on toasted slider buns, if desired.

Cold Weather Chili

Cooking Time: 30 Min

Ingredients:

- 2-3 Tbsp. butter
- 1 lb. ground beef
- 1 medium white onion, chopped
- ½ green pepper, chopped
- ½ red pepper, chopped
- 14.5 oz can pinto beans, drained
- Your favorite chili powder or pre-made chili seasoning
- One small can tomato paste
- 1 can of your favorite beer (optional) or 1½ C. beef broth
- Salt and pepper, to taste

Directions:

1. Preheat grill to 350°F. Melt butter in a large cast iron pot.
2. Add chopped onion, peppers, ground beef and pinto beans and cook for 5 minutes, covered.
3. After 5 minutes, uncover and add chili powder or seasoning. Mix well, cover and cook for 10 minutes until meat is browned.
4. Add chili paste and/or tomato paste and beer (optional, or use beef broth) and stir. Cook 15 minutes to reduce and heat through. Add salt and pepper to taste and add water if needed.
5. Serve with your favorite chili fixings! Enjoy!

The All American Burger

Cooking Time: 6 Min

Ingredients:

- ➢ 80/20 Ground Chuck- 1 Pound
- ➢ Steak- 8 ounces
- ➢ Salt
- ➢ Pepper
- ➢ Fire

Directions:

1. Cube your steak and grind together with coarse plate in the grinder.
2. Once fully ground, change the plate to a finer grind, and grind again. This will help the fat and meat combine well so that the burgers stay together.
3. Once ground, form the patties, about 4 inches.
4. Create a well in the center of the patties to help with even cooking.
5. Put the burgers in the fridge for up to 1 hour after forming the patties.
6. Fire up the grill and bring up to 400F
7. Season the patties with fresh ground black pepper and fresh ground sea salt.
8. Cook the burgers for about 4-6 minutes. Close the lid while doing this.
9. Flip once, and let cook.
10. Add cheese to the burgers and let the cheese melt over the patties.
11. Toast the bun on the grill to prevent a soggy bun when the juices of the burger comes out.
12. Once done, assemble your burger as you like and show your friends and family how you have become a true #grillionaire and that you are the KING of the cul de sac.

Chi-lanta Pork Belly Burnt Ends

Cooking Time: 4.45 Hrs

Ingredients:

- Pork Belly
- Sharp Knife
- Olive Oil
- Blues Hog Original BBQ Sauce
- Sweet Baby Rays Barbecue Sauce
- Char-Griller Grills Rib Rub
- Foil
- Butter (Not Margarine)
- Apple Juice (Non From Concentrate)
- Pan
- Drip Pan
- Baking Rack
- Golden Protective Services Nitrile Powder Free Gloves For Food Safety

Directions:

1. Prepping: Using a sharp knife slice and remove the skin and excess fat from the pork belly.
2. Slice into cubes
3. Coat with olive oil
4. Season with Char-Griller Rib Rub
5. Smoking
6. Fire up your Char-Griller Grill to 250°.
7. Place drip pan filled with water under the grill grates.
8. Place the pork belly on the baking rack.
9. Spritz every 30 minutes with Apple Juice and rotate the baking rack for even smoking.
10. After 3 hours of smoking, remove the pork belly from the baking rack and place directly in a pan with Apple Juice, Char-Griller Rib Rub, Butter & cover the pan with foil.
11. Place covered pan into the Smoker/Grill and cook for an additional 90 minutes.
12. Remove foil and discard the juices and then add BBQ sauce to the pork belly and mix.
13. Smoke uncovered for an additional 15 minutes and are done.
14. Enjoy.

Smoked Chili

Cooking Time: 2-3 Hrs

Ingredients:

- ➢ 2 lb. ground beef
- ➢ 30 oz. tomato sauce
- ➢ 30 oz. kidney beans
- ➢ 30 oz. pinto beans
- ➢ 1 C. diced onion
- ➢ ¼ C. diced green chilies
- ➢ 3 medium tomatoes chopped
- ➢ 1½ Tsp. cumin powder
- ➢ 3 Tbsp. chili powder
- ➢ 2 Tsp. black pepper
- ➢ 1 Tsp. salt
- ➢ 1 Tsp. celery salt
- ➢ 2-4 cloves garlic, minced
- ➢ ½ C. chopped cilantro
- ➢ 2 C. water

Directions:

1. Pre-heat grill to 250°F. Season ground beef with salt and pepper, to taste and brown in a cast iron pan.
2. Mix all ingredients together, add to browned ground beef and stir well to combine.
3. Smoke for 2-3 hours at 250°F, stirring every 15-20 minutes.

Grilled Ribeye Steak

Cooking Time: 8-10 Min

Ingredients:

- 1½" thick ribeye steaks
- Salt and pepper, to taste

Directions:

1. Allow the steaks to come to room temperature.
2. Pre-heat the grill to 450°F.
3. Generously season steaks on all sides with salt and pepper, or use Steak BBQ rub, to taste.
4. Place steaks on the grill and sear for 4-5 minutes on both sides. The steaks are done when internal temperature reaches 130°F for medium-rare.
5. Allow to rest for 5 minutes before slicing and serving. Enjoy!

Breakfast Burritos On The Flat Iron

Ingredients:

- ➤ Pack of 8 Breakfast Sausage Circles
- ➤ Pack of Shredded Cheese
- ➤ Burrito Tortillas (Large)
- ➤ Pack of Thick-Cut Bacon
- ➤ Dozen Eggs
- ➤ Package of Diced Frozen Hash Browns

Directions:

1. Perfect for taking on the go or preparing for the family to add some pizzazz into your mornings, these Breakfast Burritos are easy to assemble and allow you to choose toppings to make it your own.

2. Start with the hash browns on high-med/high heat with some oil. Keep an eye on them. Throw on the sausage and bacon. Cut up the sausage for the burritos. Once everything is cooked, move off to the side Warm-up a burrito to make easier to fold Ladle some eggs on to the griddle Add cheese and other toppings Remove burrito wrap Fold the egg into an omelet place on burrito wrap and fold Enjoy!

Beef Tenderloin

Ingredients:

- ➤ Beef tenderloin
- ➤ Salt and pepper, to taste

Directions:

1. Pre-heat grill to 350°
2. Place meat directly over heat
3. Grill 10-12 minutes on each side
4. Mid-rare when internal temp reaches 135°
5. Remove, and let rest for 3-5 minutes

Dry Aged Rib Roast

Cooking Time: 1.5 Hrs

Ingredients:

- 6-8 lb. dry aged rib roast
- ½ C. melted butter
- 4 sprigs of parsley
- 4 sprigs of basil
- 4 sprigs of rosemary
- Kosher salt
- Black pepper
- Paprika
- Garlic

Directions:

1. Finely chop parsley, basil, and rosemary, and mix with melted butter
2. Place rib roast on grill at 350°F over indirect heat and grill for approximately 45 minutes
3. Brush roast with buttered herbs
4. Continue to cook over indirect heat for additional 45 minutes or until internal temp reaches 145°F

Certified Creole Y not Beef N' Bacon Jerky

Cooking Time: 4 Hrs

Ingredients:

- Bottom Flat Steak- 1 Pound
- Skirt Steak- 1 Pound
- Bacon- 12 ounces
- Kikkoman Teriyaki Baste and Glaze- 11.8 ounce bottle
- Char-Griller Grills Steak Rub
- Pepper Flakes
- Olive Oil
- Large Ziplock Bag
- Fogo Charcoal The Rub
- Fogo Charcoal Eucalyptus & Premium Blends
- Apple Wood Chunks

Directions:

1. Prepping:Slice the Bottom Flat Steak & Skirt Steak into small-medium personal pieces & set aside.Tip: cut small end pieces & excess fat.

2. Pour Kikkoman Teriyaki Baste & Glaze in Ziplock Bag.

3. Apply Olive Oil & Char-griller Grills Steak Rub to both sides of the meat & place in ziplock bag.

4. Mix the meat in the Ziplock bag & place in the refrigerator for 2-24 hours.

5. Remove from fridge and place on tray and allow the meat to get to room temperature.

6. Bacon: No need to marinade. When your ready to cook apply olive oil on both sides of the bacon & season both sides with Fogo Charcoal The Rub.Tip: placing the bacon to a baking rack allows easy handing/rotating of the bacon during the cooking process.

7. Cooking:Preheat smoker/grill with charcoal & apple wood chunks to 180°-200°.Tip: don't allow temperature to rise over 200°. Add charcoal/wood chunks as needed. Low smoke is needed to help dry out the meat. Check fire about 30-45 mins.Tip: do not use a spritz because the goal is to dry out the meat.

8. It will roughly take four hours to cook the jerky. dry out the meat.

9. Jerky will be dark in color, tender & a bit crispy when completed.

10. Dry out the meat.

11. When done, remove jerky from the smoker/grill and enjoy your Beef n' Bacon Jerky throughout the week with Family & Friends.

12. Store jerky in a ziplock bag. No need to place in refrigerator but can if you like.

Crab-stuffed Grilled Flank Steak With Asparagus

Cooking Time: 30 Min

Ingredients:

- 2 lb. flank steak
- 6-8 oz. crab meat
- 4 oz. cream cheese, softened
- 1 bunch asparagus, divided
- ¼ C. parsley, chopped
- 2 Tsp. garlic powder
- 2 Tbsp. olive oil
- 2 Tsp. salt, or to taste
- 2 Tsp. pepper, or to taste

Directions:

1. Flank Steak:Remove any excess fat and sinew from the flank steak. Rinse steak and pat dry with paper towel. 2. Butterfly the flank steak lengthwise, keeping the knife parallel and stopping approximately ½ inch from the other long edge, until the meat can open like a book. 3. Generously season flank steak with salt, pepper and garlic powder. 4. Spread an even layer of cream cheese on the steak. 5. Sprinkle parsley evenly on top of the cream cheese layer. 6. Spread crab meat evenly on top of cream cheese/parsley layer.. 7. Starting at one end, roll steak and fillings tightly, and tie securely in multiple spots with kitchen twine. Snip off any excess twine. 8. Brush steak roll with olive oil, salt and pepper, flipping over to evenly coat top and bottom. 9. Place steak on direct heat at 400°F and sear for 2 minutes on each side, rotating a quarter turn each time. 10. Transfer steak to indirect heat side of grill and cook 20-25 minutes until internal temperature reaches 140-145°F. 1 Remove from the grill, allow to rest for 8-10 minutes before slicing in 1"-1½" increments. 12. Cut and remove kitchen twine before serving.
2. Asparagus:
3. Rinse asparagus spears and cut off the ends.
4. Coat lightly with olive oil and season with salt and pepper, to taste.
5. Place asparagus on the grill at 400°F and cook for 4-5 minutes.

Pastrami Swiss Burger

Ingredients:

- 2 lbs. ground beef
- ½ lb. Pastrami, sliced
- 2 eggs, beaten
- Steak BBQ rub
- 1 C. beef all-purpose sauce
- Swiss cheese, sliced
- Hamburger buns
- Condiments of choice

Directions:

1. Place ground beef in large bowl, add eggs and season with Steak BBQ rub, or your favorite rub, to taste and sauce. Mix ingredients by hand until just blended.

2. Form 1" thick patties and place on a wax paper lined tray. Place tray with patties in refrigerator and allow to chill for 10-15 minutes.

3. Place chilled patties on the grill at 350°F for 5 minutes per side, with a quarter turn halfway through for good sear marks.

4. Bush burgers with more sauce, if desired and top with sliced pastrami and cheese. Allow cheese to melt, about 1-2 minutes. Burgers are done when internal temperature reaches 165°F for medium-rare.

Steak And Shrimp On The Flat Iron

Cooking Time: 10 Min

Ingredients:

- Strip Steak
- 1 Lb Raw Shrimp
- 1 Yellow Onion
- Handfull Of Mushrooms
- Char-Griller Steak Seasoning
- Char-Griller Creole Seasoning
- 1 Stick Of Butter
- Salt and Pepper
- Garlic Powder

Directions:

1. If frozen, thaw your shrimp in the sink under running cold water. While that's going, cut up your onion and mushrooms. Prepare your steak by patting dry, adding the steak seasoning, and finally coating with some olive oil. Next, heat up your griddle to high heat for the onions/mushrooms and medium for the shrimp. Toss on the onions and mushrooms on the high heat side and the shrimp on the medium heat side. Add some butter, salt, pepper, garlic to the onions/mushrooms and the creole seasoning on the shrimp. Move them around a bit so you don't end up burning them. Remove when done. Clear your griddle and throw the steaks on the high heat. You should hear a nice sizzle. Flip every couple minutes until done to your liking. Plate it up and enjoy!

Left Over Cheesy Mac N' Smoked Brisket Meat Pies Recipe

Cooking Time: 10 Min

Ingredients:

- Left over Brisket: You Can Also Use Ground Beef 1 Pound
- Left over Mac n' Cheeses: 20 oz.
- Dough Discs: 7 (You Can Also Use Refrigerated Biscuit Dough)
- Green Pepper: 1/2 diced
- Green Onions: One Bush Chopped.
- Olive Oil: 2 Tablespoons
- Self-Rising Flour: 1 Tablespoon
- Garlic Powder: to taste.
- Shredded Cheeses: 7 oz
- Char-Griller Grills Akorn Kamado Charcoal, Black
- Fogo Eucalyptus & Premium Lump Charcoal.
- Large Cast Iron Skillet
- Lard: for Frying Quarter Skillet.

Directions:

1. Take your left over smoked brisket, green onions, green peppers, Self-Rising flour and place in a medium heated cast iron skillet with olive oil. Mix ingredients thoroughly for 15 minutes. Then set aside to cool. Spread a few sprinkles of Self-Rising Flour so the dough discs don't stick to the surface. Fill the dough discs with the smoked brisket seasoned up mixture, Mac n' Cheese and shredded Cheese. Seal the ingredients in the dough discs using a fork on one side only. Tip: you can also make some with just smoked brisket seasoned up mixture Fire up your grill, then place the cast iron skillet filled with the lard to medium heat for meat pie frying. Place Meat Pies in the cast iron skillet. Flip after 3-4 mins and then fry for an additional 4-5 minutes. Dough will turn golden brown. Remove and enjoy! Tip: you can also freeze any uncooked meat pies and fry them up another time

Brisket Hash On The Flat Iron Portable

Cooking Time: 30 Min

Ingredients:

- 1 Bag Of Frozen Shredded Hash Brown Potatoes (30 oz)
- 2 Cups Smoked Brisket (Cubed or Chopped)
- 4-6 Slices Bacon
- 1 Yellow Onion (Diced)
- 1 Red Bell Pepper (Seeded and Diced)
- 1 Green Pepper (Seeded and Diced)
- 1 Tbsp Minced Garlic
- 3 Tbsp Olive Oil
- 2 Tbsp Char-Griller Original AP Seasoning
- 2 Tsp Salt
- 1 Tsp Black Pepper
- 5-10 Large Eggs
- Optional: BBQ Sauce

Directions:

1. Heat some olive oil to grease Flat Iron Griddle Cook bacon over medium-high heat until fully cooked but not crispy, chop and set aside for later Heat more olive oil and cook onions over medium-high heat about 3 minutes, until translucent in color Add in peppers and garlic Cook for 1-2 more minutes Add in hash brown potatoes and cook for 15-20 minutes turning often to ensure all ingredients brown evenly (Add more olive oil if needed) Add in your brisket and chopped bacon, season all ingredients with the Char-Griller Original AP seasoning, salt, pepper Cook for 5-10 minutes until brisket is brown and potatoes are fully tender Remove from heat and keep warm Cook eggs as you like, sunny side up or even scrambled eggs go great with this recipe (Optional) Warm BBQ sauce in microwave for 30 seconds and stir To plate, scoop hash onto plate then top with cooked eggs and optional BBQ sauce!

Smoked Corned Beef

Ingredients:

- 3-5 Lb Corned Beef Brisket
- 1 Tbsp of Onion Powder
- 1 Tbsp of Garlic Powder
- 2 Tbsp of Paprika
- 2 Tbsp of Coriander Powder
- 2 Tbsp of Black Pepper
- 3 Tbsp of Brown Sugar

Directions:

1. Place corned beef brisket in a bowl covered with water. Refrigerate overnight, Preheat the smoker between 250-275 degrees by adding desired coals and/or wood to the Side Fire Box. If you do not own a Side Fire Box, no problem! To accomplish the same effect, simply arrange coals and/or wood opposite your cooking area. If you want to place your brisket on the right side of the grates, then arrange coals/wood on the left side, etc. Add desired wood chips to the smoker. Combine seasonings and spices in a bowl to create rub Remove the meat from the water and use paper towels to pat dry. Prepare meat by trimming excess fat if you desire. Coat the meat all over with the rub. Place meat in the smoker until the internal temperature reaches 160 degrees.(2-3 hours) Wrap the meat in butcher paper or aluminum foil and return to the smoker until the internal temperature reaches 195 degrees. (2-3 hours) Allow the meat the rest for a minimum of 30 minutes before slicing Serve warm, enjoy!

DESSERTS

Smoked Blueberry Crisp

Cooking Time: 45 Min

Ingredients:

- ➤ Blueberries - 5 Cups
- ➤ Sugar - 2 Tablespoons
- ➤ Ground Ginger - 1/2 Teaspoon
- ➤ Brown Sugar - 1/2 Cup
- ➤ Flour - 1/2 Cup
- ➤ Rolled Oats - 3/4 Cup
- ➤ Cinnamon - 1 Tablespoon
- ➤ Melted Butter - 1/2 Cup

Directions:

1. To begin, put your blueberries into a half size foil pan and spread them out evenly.

2. Mix your sugar and ground ginger and evenly coat all the blueberries.

3. Mix the remaining ingredients together and distribute evenly over the top of the blueberries.

4. Bring your AKORN Kamado up to 375 degrees with a chunk of cherry wood for smoke and the Smokin' Stone in place to set up for indirect cooking.

5. Once the smoke is a clean smoke, that is thin and blue, place your half steamer pan on the AKORN for forty minutes. After forty minutes remove from AKORN, let cool and enjoy.

Grilled Stuffed Peaches

Cooking Time: 20 Min

Ingredients:

- ➤ 1- 2 peaches per person
- ➤ 2 Tbsp. honey, divided
- ➤ 4 oz. blue cheese, or to taste
- ➤ Coarse black pepper, to taste
- ➤ 2-3 slices of bacon, for garnish

Directions:

1. Rinse peaches and dry with paper towel. Slice in half, remove stone and cut the pit hole slightly larger.

2. Fry bacon in a pan to desired crispness according to package directions, drain grease and crumble when cool. Set aside in a small bowl.

3. Place peaches cut side down directly on the grill at 350°F for 5-7 minutes, depending on the size.

4. Turn peaches over and fill holes with blue cheese and crumbled bacon and bake for 5-7 minutes, until peaches are softened and cheese is melted.

5. Remove peaches from grill, drizzle with honey and sprinkle with coarse black pepper to serve.

Grilled S'mores 4 Ways

Servings: 4

Cooking Time: 5 Min

Ingredients:

- ➢ Graham Crackers - 4 Full Crackers
- ➢ Large Marshmallows - 4
- ➢ Milk Chocolate Bar
- ➢ Dark Chocolate Bar
- ➢ Cookie Butter
- ➢ Peanut and Caramel Candy Bar
- ➢ Chili Powder
- ➢ Peanut Butter

Directions:

1. Heat grill to 350 degrees
2. Break four graham crackers in half and lay out.
3. Top the first graham cracker with milk chocolate bar and peanut butter.
4. Top the second graham cracker with milk chocolate and cookie butter
5. Top third graham cracker with dark chocolate and a sprinkle of chili powder.
6. Top fourth graham cracker with Snickers Bar cut in half longways.
7. Top each graham cracker with a marshmallow and the other half of the graham cracker.
8. Wrap each s'mores in its own foil packet.
9. Place on warming rack of the grill for 4 to 5 minutes.
10. Enjoy.

Guinness Cupcakes With Whiskey Salted Caramel Buttercream

Cooking Time: 25 Min

Ingredients:

- 1 Devils food Cake Mix
- 1 3.9 Oz Instant Chocolate Pudding
- 1 Cup Sour Cream
- 1/2 Cup Guinness
- 1/2 Cup of Oil
- 4 Eggs
- 3/4 Cup Mini Chocolate Chips
- 1 Cup of Light Brown Sugar
- 1/4 Cup of Butter
- 1/4 Cup of Milk
- 1/4 Cup of Whiskey
- 1/4 Tbsp Sea Salt
- 4 Sticks of Unsalted Butter
- 6 Cup of Powdered Sugar
- 1/4 Cup of Salted Caramel

Directions:

1. Heat Akorn to 325 for indirect heat and add liners to a cupcake pan Add cake mix, pudding, sour cream, oil, Guinness, eggs, and ½ c. of the chocolate chips in a large bowl and mix together until combined Divide batter evenly into 24 cupcakes Bake for 20 minutes or until middle of the cake springs back when gently pushed down or until a toothpick inserted into the center comes out clean While cupcakes are cooling, add brown sugar, 1/4 c. butter, milk, and sea salt to a medium sauce pan On medium heat, melt caramel mixture stirring frequently until mixture starts to simmer Allow to simmer without stirring for 5-7 minutes until thickened. Remove from heat and allow to cool To make the frosting, add butter to mixer and beat until smooth and creamy. Slowly add the powdered sugar and beat until light and fluffy. Add caramel to frosting and beat until combined Top cooled cupcakes with a spoonful of buttercream and spread across the cupcake I like to add a drizzle of the leftover caramel on top of the frosted cupcakes with a little sprinkle of the leftover chocolate chips

2. If caramel starts to thicken too much to drizzle, you can microwave it for 10 seconds

Faux Apple Pie

Ingredients:

- 3 Cups Almond Flour (Crust)
- Baking Powder - 3 Tbsp (Crust)
- 1/3 Cup Xanthan Gum (Crust)
- 1/2 Cup and 1 Tbsp Coconut Flour (Crust)
- Apple Cider Vinegar - 2 Tbsp
- 3 Eggs, Whisked (Crust)
- Water - 3 Tbsp (Crust)
- 6 Chayote Squash, peeled, cored, sliced thin (Filling)
- 1 Cup Lakanto Golden Sweetener (Filling)
- Cinnamon - 2 Tbsp (Filling)
- Nutmeg - 1 tsp (Filling)
- Vanilla - 2 Tbsp (Filling)
- Lemon Juice - 3 Tbsp (Filling)
- 1/4 Cup Lankanto Classic Granulated Sweetener (Filling)
- Butter - 3 Tbsp (Filling)
- 1 Bag Cinnamon Pecan Lollis Cookie Clusters (Topping)

Directions:

1. Mix all wet ingredients in one bowl, set aside.
2. Mix all dry ingredients in large bowl, once dry ingredients are combined, slowly add were ingredients.
3. Mix with a spoon as good as you can, then knead with hands.
4. Shape into a ball, wrap in saran wrap and refrigerate for 2 hours.
5. Combine in a sauce pan, cook over medium heat for 20 minutes.
6. Add more sweetener if desired.
7. Remove from heat to cool.
8. Roll out dough between 2 sheets of parchment paper until 1/4 inch thin, place in aluminum pie pan - trim edges.
9. Poke holes in crust with fork.
10. Preheat grill to 325-350°.
11. Place pie crust on grill over indirect heat.
12. Cook about 5-8 minutes until crust starts to turn golden.
13. Remove from grill, add pie filling and even spread the crumbled Lollis Cookie Clusters over the top until filling is covered.
14. Place pie back on grill over indirect heat for about 25-30 minutes until nicely browned.
15. Let pie cool completely before serving.
16. Pairs well with vanilla Rebel Creamery ice cream.

Akorn Cinnamon Streusel Coffee Cake

Cooking Time: 2 Hrs

Ingredients:

- 1 ½ cups all-purpose flour (Topping)
- 1 ¼ cups packed light-brown sugar (Topping)
- 1 ½ tsp ground cinnamon (Topping)
- 1 ½ sticks cold salted butter, cut into fifths (Topping)
- 1 ½ cups chopped toasted pecans (Topping)
- 1 tsp kosher salt (Topping)
- 1 ¼ tsp baking powder (Cake)
- ½ tsp baking soda (Cake)
- 1 stick salted butter (room temperature) (Cake)
- 2 cups all-purpose flour (Cake)
- 1 ¼ cup granulated sugar (Cake)
- ½ tsp kosher salt (Cake)
- 2 large eggs (Cake)
- 1 ½ tsp vanilla extract (Cake)
- 1 cup plain greek yogurt (Cake)
- 1 cup powdered sugar (Glaze)
- 2 tbsp milk (Cake)

Directions:

1. Oktoberfest doesn't have to be just brats and sauerkraut. Bryan Head, @thebbqhead, made a classic Cinnamon Streusel Coffee Cake recipe and used his AKORN to bake it!

2. Toast pecans. Preheat oven to 275°F. In a bowl, melt a half stick of salted butter and toss pecans in the butter. Lay out pecans evenly on a baking sheet and toast for one hour flipping every 15 minutes. Let cool. Chop coarsely and set aside. Make the streusel topping. Mix together flour, ¾ cup brown sugar, 1 tsp cinnamon, and 1 tsp of salt. Cut in butter with sturdy fork or rub in with your fingers until pea-sized clumps remain. Mix in ½ cup chopped pecans. Refrigerate until ready to use. Make the streusel center. Mix together remaining ½ cup brown sugar, ½ tsp cinnamon, and 1 cup pecans. Prepare AKORN for indirect heat at 325°F. Make your cake: Butter the pan. Use a 9-inch tube pan with a removable bottom for best results. Sift in flour, baking powder, baking soda, and ½ tsp salt into a mixing bowl. Beat butter and granulated sugar with a mixer on medium speed for 2 minutes. Beat in eggs, one at a time, then vanilla. Beat in flour mixture in 3 stages alternating with greek yogurt, beginning and ending with the flour. Continue to beat at medium speed until well combined. Add half the batter into the pan. Sprinkle on the streusel center mixture evenly. Add the rest of the batter and spread evenly using a spatula. Sprinkle on the streusel topping evenly over batter. Bake until cake shows golden brown and a toothpick inserted into the center comes out clean, about 1 hour. Transfer pan to a wire rack to cool. Remove cake from pan. Make the glaze: Mix together powdered sugar and milk until you get your desired consistency. Drizzle over cake and down the sides and middle. Slice and enjoy!

Cheesecake Stuffed Apples

Cooking Time: 60 Min

Ingredients:

- Medium Baking Apples (I used Pink Lady) - 4
- Softened Cream Cheese - 8 Ounces
- Egg - 1
- Sugar - 1/3 Cup
- Cinnamon - 1/4 Teaspoon
- Crushed Graham Crackers - 1/4 Cup
- Prepared Caramel Sauce for Garnish

Directions:

1. Light AKORN and heat to 325
2. Cut bottoms of apples just enough to make them stand up straight
3. Hollow out apples with an apple corer or melon baller. Leave a ¼ inch of flesh around sides and bottom
4. Mix cream cheese, egg, sugar, vanilla, and cinnamon together until smooth
5. Spoon cream cheese mixture into each apple, leaving 1/2 inch space at the top
6. Sprinkle tops with graham crackers
7. Place apples in a small aluminum pan and place on grill
8. Allow to bake for 50-60 minutes. Filling should look semi set and apples should be soft
9. Allow to cool at room temperature then place in refrigerator until cold
10. Before serving, drizzle with caramel sauce

Strawberry And Rhubarb Crumble Pie

Cooking Time: 35-40 Min

Ingredients:

- 1¼ C. and ¾ C. all-purpose flour, plus 2 Tbsp. for filling
- 1 C. unsalted butter, diced and divided
- 1 C. sugar
- ½ C. light brown sugar
- 1 large egg
- 2 C. fresh rhubarb, cut into ½" dice
- 2 C. fresh strawberries, stemmed and sliced
- ¼ Tsp. orange zest, finely grated, optional
- 2 Tbsp. cold water, or more as needed
- 1 Tsp. vanilla extract
- Cold water, as needed

Directions:

1. Add 1¼ C. flour and salt to a large bowl and cut in ½ C. of butter with a pastry blender until the mixture resembles coarse crumbs. 2. Gradually add cold water to crumb mixture, until dough holds together when pressed. 3. Shape into a ball and wrap in plastic. Refrigerate 30 minutes. 4. Turn dough onto a floured surface and roll into a circle large enough to cover a buttered pie dish. Place dough into pie dish, trim the edges and prick the bottom with a fork.

2. Crumble Topping

3. In a medium bowl, combine ¾ C. flour, light brown sugar, and remaining ½ C. of butter Mix using a pastry blender or electric mixer until it resembles coarse crumbs.

4. Filling:Pre-heat grill to 400°F. In a large bowl, whisk 2 Tbsp. flour, egg, 1 C. sugar and vanilla together, until sugar is dissolved. 2. Add strawberries and rhubarb and mix until just blended. Let stand for 30 minutes at room temperature. 3. After 30 minutes, pour filling into pie crust. Sprinkle crumble topping evenly over pie and cover loosely with foil. Bake at 400°F for 35-40 minutes or until filling is bubbly and crumble topping is golden brown. Remove foil during the last 10 minutes.

5. Cool on wire rack before slicing and serving.

Skillet Brownie On The Grill

Ingredients:

- ➢ Softened Butter- 2 Tablespoons
- ➢ Heavy Whipping Cream- 1 Tablespoon
- ➢ Large Egg- 1
- ➢ Erythritol Blend (or Sweeter of Your Choice)- 3 Tablespoons
- ➢ Cocoa Powder- 2.5 Tablespoons
- ➢ Almond Flour- 2.5 Tablespoons
- ➢ Pinch of Sea Salt

Directions:

1. Preheat the grill to 350°.

2. Mix together all of the ingredients until smooth and spread the batter in a greased mini cast iron skillet.

3. Place the skillet directly on the preheated grill grate, close the grill, and bake for 6 to 8 minutes—or just until set. Do not over bake in the grill, as the hot skillet will continue to bake the brownie as it sits.

4. Top with sugar free vanilla ice cream, sugar free chocolate syrup, and a sliced strawberry. Serve warm.

5. This serves one to two, but can be doubled or tripled for more servings. Bake each batch in its own mini skillet.

Chocolate Lava Cake

Cooking Time: 15 Min

Ingredients:

- ½ C. all-purpose flour
- 1 stick unsalted butter
- 2 oz. bittersweet chocolate
- 2 oz. semisweet chocolate
- 1¼ C. powdered sugar
- 2 eggs and 3 egg yolks
- 1 Tsp. vanilla extract

Directions:

1. Pre-heat grill to 425°F. Spray four 6 oz. ramekins with baking spray and place on a baking sheet.
2. Melt the butter, bittersweet chocolate and semisweet chocolate together in a pan on medium heat, stirring constantly. Stir in the sugar until dissolved.
3. Whisk in the eggs and egg yolks, then add vanilla. Gradually stir in flour. Divide the mixture among the ramekins.
4. Bake until the sides are firm and the centers are soft, about 15 minutes. Let stand 1 minute.
5. To serve, plate each cake while warm and serve with vanilla ice cream.

Smoked White Chocolate Christmas Candy

Cooking Time: 1 Hrs

Ingredients:

- 3 Cups Cheerios
- 3 Cups Corn Chex
- 3 Cups Peanut Butter Chex
- 1 Cup Butter Snaps Pretzels
- 1.5 Cups M&Ms
- 32 oz white Chocolate Chips

Directions:

1. Smoke white chocolate chips using your Char-Griller Offset charcoal smoker.

2. Add 6 lit charcoals to the far side of firebox along with a mild smoking wood chunk. Maple wood goes well with this recipe. Feel free to leave vents fully open.

3. You will need 2 foil baking pans. Fill pan number one with a layer of ice cubes. About ¼ of the way full. Add white chocolate chips to the second pan. Place pan with white chocolate on top of the pan with the ice.

4. Place stacked pans in cooking chamber of your smoker. Keep as far away from fire box side as possible.

5. Smoke for 30-45 minutes. For a milder smoke flavor try 30 minutes. To impart a stronger smoke flavor, try 45 minutes.

6. Melt white chocolate over heat source.

7. Add white chocolate to a large saucepan or keep in foil pan.

8. Over medium heat or lit coals, melt until white chocolate is a smooth consistency able to be drizzled. Be sure to stir often and do not over melt.

9. In a large mixing bowl or 2 foil pans, combine dry ingredients (cheerios, corn chex, peanut butter chex, pretzels, and m&m's) making sure to evenly distribute the ingredients.

10. Drizzle white chocolate on the dry mixture. Stir in making sure to coat all the mixture in the white chocolate.

11. Lay out on parchment paper or leave in foil pans as a nice thin layer to dry/cool for 1 hour.

12. Break into small to medium pieces and enjoy!

13. This stores well in the fridge and the freezer!

Smoked Chocolate Chip Cookies

Cooking Time: 15 To 20 Min

Ingredients:

- 2.25 Cups All Purpose Flour
- 2 Sticks of Butter
- 1 tsp Salt
- 1/2 Cup Sugar
- 1 Cup Light Brown Sugar
- 3 tsp Baking Powder
- 2 Eggs
- 1 tsp Vanilla Extract
- 2 Tbsp Milk
- Chocolate Chips (Your Choice with How Much)
- Chopped Pecans (Your Choice How Much)

Directions:

1. Melt the butter in a small pan.
2. Sift the flour, salt, & baking powder into a bowl.
3. Pour the butter in a mixing bowl & cream with the white & brown sugars.
4. Add the eggs, milk, and vanilla to the creamed sugar & mix.
5. Slowly add the flour mixture to the wet ingredients, beating constantly.
6. Mix in the chocolate chips & pecans.
7. Place the cookie dough in the fridge for a minimum of 30 minutes.
8. Heat your Char-griller Smoker/Grill to 350° or you can bake them in an oven at the same temperature.
9. Using a spoon make the cookies into a ball shape and place on pizza stone or cookie sheet using parchment paper or peach butcher paper.
10. Place in smoker/grill and smoke for 15-20 minutes or until golden brown.
11. Remove the cookies from the smoker/grill and allow them to cool for 10 minutes.
12. Enjoy.

Plum Galette

Cooking Time: 45-50 Min

Ingredients:

- 1½ C. and 3 Tbsp. all-purpose flour
- 1 ½ sticks unsalted butter, cut into ½" pieces
- ¼ Tsp. salt
- 1/3 C. ice water
- ¼ C. plus 1/3 C. sugar, reserve 1 Tsp.
- 3 Tbsp. ground almonds
- 2½ lbs. large plums, halved, pitted and cut into ½" wedges
- ½ C. good-quality plum preserves, strained if chunky or seedy
- Corn meal, for dusting

Directions:

1. Put 1½ C. flour, butter and salt into a food processor and mix for 5 seconds. 2. Add ice water and mix for 5 seconds longer, just until the dough holds together. Small pieces of butter should still be visible. 3. Remove the dough and gather it into a ball. On a lightly floured surface, roll out the dough into a large circle, 1/8" thick. 4. Drape the dough over the rolling pin and transfer to a large baking sheet. Refrigerate the dough until firm, 10-20 minutes. 5. While dough is chilling, pre-heat grill to 400°. In a small bowl, combine ¼ C. of the sugar with the ground almonds and 3 Tbsp. flour and mix well. Spread evenly over the dough to within 2" of the edge. 6. Arrange plum wedges on top and dot with butter. Sprinkle 1/3 C. sugar over the fruit. Fold the edge of the dough up over the plums to create a 2" border.

2. Tip: If the dough feels cold and firm when folding up the edges, wait a few minutes until it softens to prevent cracking.

3. Sprinkle the border with the remaining 1 Tsp. sugar. 7. Transfer the galette to a pre-heated pizza stone dusted with corn meal to prevent sticking, and bake at 400°F for 45-50 minutes, until the fruit is very soft and the crust is golden brown. 8. Remove from the grill and evenly brush the preserves over the hot fruit.

4. Allow the galette to cool before slicing and serving. Enjoy!

Glazed Oatmeal Raisin Cookies

Cooking Time: 15 Min

Ingredients:

- ➢ 2 C. oats
- ➢ 2 C. all-purpose flour
- ➢ 1 Tbsp. baking powder
- ➢ 2 Tsp. cinnamon
- ➢ ½ Tsp. nutmeg
- ➢ 1 Tsp. salt
- ➢ 2 sticks unsalted butter, softened
- ➢ 1 C. sugar
- ➢ ½ C. brown sugar
- ➢ 2 eggs
- ➢ ½ C. raisins
- ➢ 1 C. powdered sugar
- ➢ 1 Tbsp. vanilla extract
- ➢ 2-3 Tbsp. milk

Directions:

1. Pre-heat grill to 350°F. 2. In a medium bowl combine the oats, flour, baking powder, cinnamon, nutmeg, and salt. Mix well and set aside. 3. In a large bowl whisk the butter, sugar, and brown sugar together until sugar is dissolved. Add in the eggs one at a time, stirring well until combined. 4. Add the oat mixture to the butter mixture and stir until combined. Fold in the raisins. 5. Drop 1 Tbsp. of cookie batter onto cookie sheets, 2" apart. Bake 15 minutes or until the edges are golden brown. Remove from grill and transfer to a wire rack to cool. 6. While cookies are cooling, prepare icing by combining the powdered sugar and vanilla in a bowl. Gradually add in milk until mixture is thick but spreadable.

2. Dunk the top of each cookie into the icing and let the excess drip off. Serve warm.

Salted Caramel Chocolate Tart

Cooking Time: 20 Min

Ingredients:

- 1- 8 oz Bag of Sea Salt Kettle Potato Chips, Crushed (Crust)
- 1/4 Cup Flour (Crust)
- 5 Tbsp Unsalted Butter, Melted (Crust)
- 1 Cup Sugar (Caramel)
- 1/2 Cup Heavy Cream (Caramel)
- 6 Tbsp Unsalted Butter (Caramel)
- 1 tsp Sea Salt (Caramel)
- 10 Oz Semisweet Chocolate Chips (Chocolate Layer)
- 1/4 Cup Heavy Cream (Chocolate Layer)
- 1/4 Cup Sugar (Chocolate Layer)
- 2 tsp Vanilla Extract (Chocolate Layer)
- 2 Large Eggs (Chocolate Layer)

Directions:

1. Light grill for indirect heat and heat to 350.
2. In a large bowl, combine crushed chips, melted butter, and flour. Mix until combined.
3. Press into tart pan and place on grill. Bake for 15 minutes.
4. Remove from grill and allow to cool.
5. In a sauce pan over medium heat, add sugar and allow to melt completely, stirring frequently.
6. Add cream and butter, stir until combined.
7. Add sea salt and allow to boil for 5 minutes.
8. Remove from heat and allow to cool for 15 minutes.
9. Pour caramel onto crust.
10. In a saucepan over medium heat, add cream and allow to heat up.
11. Add chocolate chips and sugar, stir until melted and smooth.
12. Add eggs one at a time stirring until combined.
13. Add vanilla and stir.
14. Pour chocolate until crust.
15. Place tart on grill and allow to bake for 20 minutes.
16. Remove from grill and let cool.

Candied Bacon Scones With Bourbon Glaze

Cooking Time: 15 Min

Ingredients:

- All Purpose Flour - 3 Cups
- Salt - 3/4 tsp
- Baking Powder - 1 Tbsp
- Sugar - 1/3 cup
- Cinnamon - 1/2 tsp
- Vanilla Extract - 1.5 tsp
- Heavy Cream - 1.5 Cups
- Chopped Bacon - 1/3 cup
- Heavy Cream - 1/4 cup

Directions:

1. Look here for the Candied Bacon Recipe and here for the Bourbon Glaze Recipe.

2. Have the Candied Bacon and Bourbon Glaze Ready nearby. Whisk together flour, salt, baking powder, sugar, and cinnamon. Add 1 1/2 c. cream, vanilla, candied bacon, and stir to combine. Divide dough in half. Flour a cutting board and pat each half into a 6" circle. Brush each circle of dough with the remaining cream. Place dough on parchment paper and cut into 6 triangles. Pull each wedge apart slightly and place in the freezer for 10 minutes. Transfer scones on the parchment paper to the grill grates. Bake for 15 minutes or until golden brown. Remove from grill and allow to cool. Using a 1/4 measuring cup, pour glaze over each scone and top with remaining chopped bacon.

Puffy Pancake With Fruit Compote

Cooking Time: 15 Min

Ingredients:

- 4 large eggs
- 1 C. all-purpose flour
- 1 C. milk
- 2 Tbsp. granulated sugar
- ¼ Tsp. salt
- 2 Tbsp. butter
- 2 ripe bananas, peeled and sliced
- 1 pint blueberries
- 1 Tbsp. granulated sugar
- 1 Tbsp. lemon juice
- Confectioners' sugar

Directions:

1. Pre-heat grill to 425ºF, place a 10" cast iron skillet on grill and heat until very hot.
2. In a blender at medium speed, blend eggs, milk, flour, sugar, and salt together until smooth.
3. Remove skillet from the grill, add butter and swirl until melted. Pour batter into hot skillet and bake for 15 minutes until puffy and golden brown on the edges.
4. In a large bowl, toss bananas and blueberries with sugar and lemon juice to make compote.
5. Spoon compote onto pancake and sprinkle with confectioner's sugar. To serve, cut into wedges.

PORK

Certified Pork Butt

Cooking Time: 12-20 Hrs

Ingredients:

- 2 Pork butts (6-10 lbs. each)
- Apple juice
- Your favorite rub/seasoning
- Mustard

Directions:

1. Remove the pork butt from the plastic wrap & pat dry using a paper towel.
2. Tip: Choose a pork butt with a full fat cap. This helps the meat while it's smoking for a long period of time.
3. Trim the excess fat that is loose and pulls up easily. Score the fat cap 1/8 to 1/4-inch-deep diagonally, spaced out 1/2 to 1 inch apart.
4. Tip: Scoring the meat allows the seasoning and smoke to penetrate into the pork butt.
5. Fill the marinade injector with apple juice and inject into the top and sides of the meat.
6. Spread a coating of mustard using a basting brush all over the pork butt.
7. Tip: This allows the rub to stick to the pork butt.
8. Generously season the pork butt on all sides with your favorite rub.
9. Tip: After seasoning, wrap in Saran Wrap and store in refrigerator overnight or 8-10 hours. This allows the rubs to penetrate and apple juice to tenderizer the pork butt.
10. Chef's Note: I used a combination of the Char-Griller Original All-Purpose BBQ Rub, Char-Griller Ribs BBQ Rub, TexJoy Butt & Rib Tickler Pork Rub, Barker BBQ All Purpose House Blend Rub and Southside Market Barbecue Oak Smoked Black Pepper, Coarse Ground
11. Cooking Directions
12. Ignite charcoal and preheat smoker to 225°F.
13. Add boiling water to the drip pan and place under grill grate.
14. Tip: This will add moisture for the cook and collect the drippings .
15. Smoke the pork butts f or 2 hours per pound at 225°F, until the meat reaches an internal temperature of 160°F.

16. Tip: Maintain a 225°F temperature, check fire hourly or when needed. Also spritz with apple juice every time you add fuel to your fire. Spritzing adds moisture and flavor. It prevents the pork butt from drying out and helps to create the bark. Monitor the temperature using a folding probe thermometer and/or remote thermometer.

17. Chef's Note: I used Fogo Eucalyptus Lump Charcoal for the heat and Mesquite mini logs for the smoke. Always keep the smoke stack vent open to allow the smoke to flow over the meat. Maintain the heat of smoker by adjusting the side vent on the fire box. Slightly close it if your fire gets too hot.

18. Remove the pork butts from the smoker and double wrap in foil. Before closing the wrap, add 1 C. apple juice and 1 stick of butter for each pork butt, more seasoning and BBQ sauce, to taste.

19. Place back in smoker and cook until the pork butt reaches an internal temperature of 199°F, then remove from the smoker.

20. Tip: Wrap pork butt in a large towel and place in a cooler or just set to the side for a minimum of 1-2 hours for resting. This allows the meat to cook down and stop cooking and is a major key in the process.

21. After resting, remove the towel and foil. Pull apart the pork using two forks or meat claws.

22. Make pulled pork sandwiches and endless pulled pork dishes. Enjoy!

Flavor Pro Smoked Pork Shoulder

Cooking Time: 90 Minutes Per Pound And Then 1 Hour Rest Hrs

Ingredients:

- 5 to 6 Pound Bone-In Pork Shoulder or Boston Butt
- Char-Griller Rib Rub
- Spray Bottle Full of Apple Juice and Oil

Directions:

1. Trim excess fat from the pork shoulder. (Skip this step if it is Boston Butt.) Score the remaining fat with a sharp knife.
2. Rub a liberal amount of Rib Spice Rub on the pork. Make sure each side is evenly coated.
3. Place pork in the fridge for at least 12 hours.
4. Remove pork from fridge one hour before placing on the grill.
5. Cover the left-most and center Wood Product Zones of the Flavor Drawer with foil to catch the grease.
6. Place 15 to 20 charcoal briquettes in the far right side of the Flavor Drawer.
7. Turn the burners on high and ignite. Allow the briquettes to fully ash over.
8. Once the briquettes have ashed over, add two to three wood chunks to the charcoal.
9. To Use a Log: Place a log of no more than 3 inches in diameter and 7 inches long the right-most wood product zone. Light using the right most burner.
10. The log should take about 5 to 6 minutes to ignite.
11. After the log has ignited, turn off the gas burner and allow the grill to preheat.
12. Using a Grilling Glove, adjust the smokestacks until the internal temperature of the pit holds steady at 225.
13. Place the pork over the foil and close the grill.
14. Baste pork with Apple juice every 30 to 60 minutes.
15. Make sure to keep an eye on the pit temperature. Add another log every hour or so.
16. Smoke until internal temperature is 195 to 210 degrees Fahrenheit and remove from grill.
17. Tip: If your pork shoulder hits the dreaded "stall" (won't get above 165 degrees Fahrenheit or starts dropping, wrap it in foil, add some apple juice and place back on the grill. This will get it going again.
18. Allow pork to rest for 30 minutes to an hour for best results.

Flavor Pro Quick And Easy Grilled Pork Tenderloin

Ingredients:

- 2 Pork Tenderloin
- 2 tsp Paprika
- 1 tsp Garlic Powder
- 1 tsp Cilantro
- 1 tsp Oregano
- Salt and Pepper to Taste
- Olive Oil

Directions:

1. Blend spices together in a bowl. Rub pork with olive oil and then season liberally on both sides with spice blend.

2. Set up the Flavor Pro for direct cooking. Ignite burners and turn to medium high.

3. Place pork on the grill and cook for 8 to 10 minutes per side or until the internal temperature reads 165 degrees.

4. Remove from grill and let rest for 10 minutes.

Father's Day Baby Back Ribs

Cooking Time: 6 Hrs

Ingredients:

- ➢ 1 C. warmed honey
- ➢ 1/2 C. yellow or Dijon mustard
- ➢ 2 oz. brown sugar
- ➢ 1 oz smoked paprika
- ➢ 1 Tbsp. black pepper
- ➢ 1 Tsp. crushed red pepper flakes
- ➢ 2 C. water
- ➢ 2 oz chipotle peppers

Directions:

1. Mix mustard and honey in small bowl
2. Pour over ribs and coat evenly
3. Mix together brown sugar, black pepper, red pepper flakes, and paprika in a bowl
4. Coat ribs generously with the rub mix
5. Wrap in aluminum foil and leave in the refrigerator for 24 hours
6. Pre heat grill to 275° F
7. Mix 2 C. of water and 2 oz. of chipotle peppers in a cast iron skillet
8. Baste with liquid in skillet every hour
9. Smoke for about 6 hours or until internal temperature reaches 175° F

Grilled Pork And Sweet Potato Verde Chili

Cooking Time: 3.5 Hrs

Ingredients:

- 2 Lbs Pork
- 2 Large Sweet Potatoes - Diced
- 3 Ears of Corn on the Cob
- 1 Bunch Cilantro - Stems Cut from Leaves and Set Aside
- 2 Cloves of Garlic
- 3 Tbsp Ground Cumin
- 1/2 Cup olive Oil or Avocado Oil
- 2 Cups Salsa Verde
- 6 Cups Chicken Stock
- 1 Can White Beans
- Salt and Pepper to taste
- Garnish: Cilantro, Radish, Red Onion, and/or Sour Cream

Directions:

1. Remove stems from fresh cilantro, and add to blender with garlic cloves, oil, cumin, and a pinch of s&p. Pulse until smooth and combined.

2. Preheat Char-Griller to high heat, I recommend charcoal for this recipe as it will add even more flavor.

3. In a large bowl, transfer corn, pork, and sweet potato pieces. Pour blended marinade over the ingredients and toss to combine. Once grill is heated, add all to grill, and cook until charred on each side, 6-8 mins per side. Remove and set aside.

4. Once the grilled items are cool to the touch, dice sweet potatoes and pork into similar sized pieces, and cut corn off the cob. Transfer these items to a soup pot, adding salsa verde, & chicken stock. Bring to a simmer over low.

5. Add ½ cup chopped cilantro leaves, the white beans, and S&P to taste. Simmer on low partially covered for 3 hours, until pork is fall apart tender, and chili has thickened. Serve with garnishes of choice and enjoy! Leftover Chili can stay in the fridge for up to 7 days, and frozen for 6 months.

Quick And Easy Grilled Pork Tenderloin

Cooking Time: 25 Min

Ingredients:

- 1 Pork Tenderloin
- 1 Tsp Paprika
- 1/2 Tsp Garlic Powder
- 1/2 Tsp Cilantro
- 1/2 Tsp Oregano
- Salt and Pepper to Taste
- Olive Oil

Directions:

1. Blend spices together in a bowl. Rub pork with olive oil and then season liberally on both sides with spice blend. Set up the Flavor Pro™ for direct cooking. Ignite burners and turn to medium high. Place pork on the grill and cook for 8 to 10 minutes per side or until the internal temperature reads 165 degrees. Remove from grill and let rest for 10 minutes.

Pork Belly Burnt Ends On The Akorn

Cooking Time: 2 Hrs

Ingredients:

- Slab of Pork Belly
- BBQ Rub
- 1 Stick Butter
- 1/2 Cup Brown Sugar
- Honey
- BBQ sauce
- 8 oz Apple Juice

Directions:

1. Remove skin from pork belly Cut up pork belly in 5" squares Set smoker to 250-275F - indirect - add cherry wood Place cubed pork belly pieces on smoker - cook for 1.5-2 hours Place pork belly in aluminum pan - pour in brown sugar, honey and pads of your butter Cover, and place in smoker for another 1.5-2hrs (until about 205F) Grab a new pan.. drizzle with glaze(4 oz apple juice 1 cup of bbq sauce) and shake up so they're covered Return pieces to smoker, uncovered for approx 5-10 mins until tacky Enjoy!

Flavor Pro Pork Steaks

Cooking Time: 12 Min

Ingredients:

- 4 Large Pork Steaks
- 1 Cup Stout Beer
- 2 Tbsp Canola Oil
- 3 Tbsp Minced Garlic
- 1/4 Cup Soy Sauce
- 2 Tbsp Worcestershire Sauce
- 1/3 Cup Packed Brown Sugar
- 2 tsp Hot Sauce
- 1 Tbsp Dijon Mustard
- 1 tsp Onion Powder
- 2 tsp Salt
- 2 tsp Pepper

Directions:

1. Add all ingredients to your favorite food-safe marinade container or ziplock bag along with the pork steaks.

2. Massage marinade into the steaks to ensure an even coating.

3. Store the container in the refrigerator for at least 2 hours but storing overnight is optimal.

4. Prepare the Flavor Pro for direct heat grilling (High, 400°F+) For best results, fill all three zones of the Flavor Drawer with charcoal and add a few wood chunks for added smoke flavor. Turn all four gas burners on high to ignite the coals, once the coals are fully lit, turn off the gas completely. Leave both smoke stacks fully open.

5. Remove pork steaks from the marinade and place them on the grill directly over the coals.

6. Cook for 4-6 minutes per side.

Bbq Pork Spare Ribs

Ingredients:

- ➤ Slab of Ribs- 1
- ➤ Mustard- 1/4 Cup
- ➤ Char Griller Rib Rub- 4 Tablespoon
- ➤ Butter- 1 Stick
- ➤ Apple Cider Vinegar- 1/2 Cup
- ➤ Jack Stack BBQ Seasoning- 6 Tablespoons
- ➤ G Hughes Sweet & Spicy BBQ Sauce (or Preferred BBQ Sauce)- 2/3 Cup

Directions:

1. Pat the ribs dry with a paper towel & tear off the membrane.
2. Rub a layer of mustard over the ribs.
3. Rub the ribs down with Char-Griller Rib Rub (to taste).
4. Rub the ribs down with Jack Stack BBQ seasoning (to taste).
5. Marinate for an hour.
6. Smoke ribs around 225° for 3 hours, bone side down uncovered.
7. Wrap in foil with butter & apple cider vinegar, smoke for 2 more hours.
8. Remove foil & brush with BBQ sauce & place on grill grate bone side down for 1 more hour basting occasionally.

Asian Pork Belly Skewers

Cooking Time: 2 Hrs

Ingredients:

- ➢ Pork Belly Cut into 1 1/2" Cubes - 2 Pounds
- ➢ Pineapple Cut into 1 1/2" Cubes - 1
- ➢ Char-Griller Rib Rub
- ➢ Skewers Soaked in Water
- ➢ Chopped Green Onions and Sesame Seeds - For Garnish
- ➢ Chili Garlic Sauce - 1 Tablespoon
- ➢ Rice Wine Vinegar - 1 Teaspoon
- ➢ Chopped Garlic - 1 Teaspoon
- ➢ Orange Zest - 1 Teaspoon
- ➢ Soy Sauce - 2 Teaspoons

Directions:

1. Light grill for indirect heat
2. In a large bowl, toss pork belly with rub until generously coated
3. Skewer pineapple and pork belly, alternating between the two
4. Please skewers on the grill
5. Rotate skewers after an hour
6. Meanwhile, place all sauce ingredients in a small sauce pan
7. Chili Garlic Sauce Rice Wine Vinegar Chopped Garlic Range Zest Soy Sauce Honey Ground Ginger
8. Bring the sauce to a simmer and allow to cook until thickened. Approximately 15 minutes
9. Allow to cool
10. After two hours, brush the skewers with sauce. Allow the sauce to set for approximately 30 minutes
11. When ready to serve, sprinkle with sesame seeds and green onions

Flat Iron Griddle Breakfast Sandwich

Cooking Time: 5 Min

Ingredients:

- 2 Cups Of Kodiak Cakes Pancake And Waffle Mix
- 2 Cups Of Water
- 6 Eggs
- Egg Rings
- Syrup
- 1 Pack Of Bacon

Directions:

1. Mix pancake and waffle mix with water until the mix is no longer lumpy. Place egg rings on griddle and pour pancake batter into the egg rings , add a little swirl of syrup while batter is cooking. Once the batter has a nice bubble to it remove the egg ring and flip the griddle cake. Scramble or fry your eggs and cook the bacon , construct sandwich and enjoy

Certified Grilled And Smoked Baby Back Ribs

Cooking Time: 2 1/2 Hrs

Ingredients:

- Full Slabs of Spare Ribs.
- Hot Sauce
- Favorite BBQ Rub
- Favorite BBQ Sauce
- Apple Juice (Non Concentrate)

Directions:

1. Trimming
2. Using a sharp knife slice remove any meat loose on the ends of the ribs. Also remove any access fat from top/meat side of the ribs.Tip: If you can pull any fat, you should remove it.
3. Flip the ribs over so the bones are facing up. Remove the membrane and discard. Remove any access fat.
4. Seasoning
5. Begin by leaving the the ribs bone side up. Apply coating of hot sauce for a binder.Tip: don't apply hot sauce or rubs on the sides of the ribs. This helps the exposed bones from getting burnt during the smoking process.
6. Apply even coating of BBQ rubs on the ribs.
7. Flip ribs to the top/meat side of the ribs. Apply coating of hot sauce for a binder.Tip: seasoning the bottom of the ribs first will help prevent the top/meat side seasonings from being messy.
8. Apply an even coating of BBQ rub on the top of the ribs.
9. Ribs are ready to be Smoked.
10. Grilling & Smoking
11. Grill the ribs for 2 minutes on the meat side down on the grill grill grate. Reverse them after one minute.
12. Flip the ribs so they meat side is facing up and grill for an additional 1-2 minutes.
13. Using your Char-Griller Grill glove and grill grate lifter, lift the grill grate and move off to the side of the grill. Quickly insert the Char-Griller Akorn Smokin' stone, insert Char-Griller grill drip pan filled with water, place grill grate with meat back in the pit.
14. Shut the top smoke stack to a low setting and dodge same to the bottom of the vent. This will allow you to quickly lower your fire. Lock in the temperature when it hits temperature 325°-350° by adjusting the smoke stack and bottom vent.
15. Spritz with apple juice every 30 minutes and rotate ribs.
16. After smoking for 2 1/2 hours coat ribs with BBQ sauce and smoke for an additional 20 minutes.
17. Remove Ribs and allow to rest for 15 minutes. Slice and enjoy.

Gravity 980 Smoked Pork Shoulder

Cooking Time: 3-4 Hrs

Ingredients:

- 1 7-9 Lb. Pork Shoulder, trimmed
- 3 Tbsp of Yellow Mustard
- 2 Tbsp Kosher Salt
- 2 Tbsp Black Pepper
- 2 Tbsp Garlic Powder
- 2 Tbsp Onion Powder
- 1 Tbsp Paprika
- 1 Tbsp Cumin
- 1 Cup of Apple Juice or Apple Cider Vinegar
- 1/2 Cup of Water

Directions:

1. No more babysitting your pork shoulder with the Gravity 980. Easily prepare an awesome pork shoulder for stellar dishes like sandwiches, mac and cheese or even nachos.

2. In a small bowl, combine seasonings, and in a spray, bottle combine apple cider/juice and water. Thoroughly rub mustard all over the surface of your pork shoulder then coat with all the seasonings. Remove the fire shutter from your Gravity 980 then light and load the hopper. Set the temperature to 225-250°F. Place your pork shoulder on the grill, close the lid and smoke it for 3 hours without opening the lid. Spray the shoulder generously with spray bottle mixture then continue to do so every hour for the next 3-4 hours until the shoulder reaches 200-205°F. Optionally, once the fat on top splits open, you may wrap the shoulder in butcher paper or aluminum foil for the duration of the cook. Remove from the smoker and allow it to rest for 1 hour before removing the bone and shredding. Enjoy!

Orange Pork Belly Burnt Ends

Cooking Time: 4 Hrs

Ingredients:

- Pork Belly (2-3 Lbs)
- 1 Tsp Kosher Salt
- 1/2 Tsp Coarse Black Pepper
- 1/2 Tsp Garlic Powder
- 1 Disposable Aluminum Pan
- 1/2 Cup Orange Juice (For Spritzing)
- Hickory Wood (Splits or Chunks)
- 1/2 Cup White Sugar
- 1 Tbsp Soy Sauce
- 2 Tbsp Rice Vinegar
- 1 Tsp Sesame Oil
- 1/4 Tsp Ginger Powder
- 1/4 Tsp Garlic Powder
- 1/2 Tsp Red Chili Flakes

Directions:

1. Cut the pork belly into 1-1 ½ inch cubes. Combine salt, pepper, and garlic powder in a small bowl and season the pork belly cubes on all sides. Whisk together all the orange sauce ingredients in a medium size bowl and place in the refrigerator for later use.

2. Heat your smoker to a temperature of 275 F. Place the pork belly cubes into the side of the smoker that is furthest away from the fire. Spritz every 40-45 minutes until the pork belly starts to read an internal temp between 190 F – 200 F. *Tip* Place a water pan inside the smoker next to the fire box to help with added moisture.

3. Place the pork belly cubes in an aluminum pan and add the orange sauce mixture. Return the pan into the smoker maintaining 275 F.

4. Once the orange sauce has reduced and the cubes look caramelized it is time to pull from the smoker (This should take approximately 25-35 minutes). Top with sesame seeds and green onions. Enjoy!

Ultimate Pork Belly Sliders

Cooking Time: 2:15 Hrs

Ingredients:

- 4 lb. pork belly
- Yellow mustard
- Original All-Purpose BBQ rub, to taste
- Your favorite sweet BBQ rub, to taste
- Hawaiian sweet rolls or your favorite roll for sliders
- Your favorite toppings
- Your favorite BBQ sauce

Directions:

1. Remove the skin from the pork belly and season the top generously with a layer of yellow mustard, followed by Original All-Purpose BBQ rub and your favorite sweet BBQ sauce, to taste.

2. Pre-heat grill to 275°F for indirect heat with a Smokin' Stone. Allow the belly to smoke for 2 hours or until internal temperature reaches 175°F. Remove the belly from the grill and allow to rest.

3. After removing the pork belly and Smokin' Stone, stir the charcoal and open up both vents to allow the grill to reach maximum temperature for searing.

4. While the grill is heating up, slice the pork belly into ¼" thick strips and arrange on the grill. Work in batches if needed. Fry the belly for 3 minutes on each side, to allow the fat to render. Season the belly with BBQ rub again, if desired.

5. Slice the pack of Hawaiian sweet rolls in half and arrange the pork belly on the bottom half. Cover with the top half and brush with melted butter and garlic, if desired. Place the rolls in a large pan and back onto the grill to crisp up for 10 minutes.

6. Remove the pan from the grill and allow the rolls to cool slightly before slicing into individual sliders. Add your favorite toppings and sauce and enjoy!

Chipotle Orange Glazed Bacon Wrapped And Stuffed Pork Loin

Cooking Time: 2 Hrs

Ingredients:

- 1-1½ lb. pork tenderloins
- 1 lb. bacon
- 1 C. spicy honey BBQ sauce
- 1 C. sweet orange marmalade
- 1 Tbsp. crushed fresh garlic, to taste
- 1 Tbsp. Chipotle chili powder, to taste
- 3 Tbsp. pork rub or preferred seasoning

Directions:

1. Combine BBQ sauce, marmalade, garlic and Chipotle chili powder in a saucepan on the stove until heated through, 3-5 minutes or until all ingredients are well blended. 2. Mix well and turn heat to low until ready to use. 3. Stir occasionally and refrigerate leftovers.

2. Pork tenderloin

3. Generously season pork tenderloins with rub and layer 2-3 strips of bacon on top. 2. Evenly spread a ¼ of the Chipotle orange glaze over the bacon layer. Tie securely in multiple spots with kitchen twine. Snip off any excess twine. 4. Lay out remaining bacon in a basket weave pattern on a cutting board. 5. Wrap the pork tenderloin, tucking ends under and season with rub. 6. Place bacon wrapped tenderloin to smoke on the indirect side of the grill at 225°F for 2 hours. 7. Brush the remaining Chipotle orange glaze onto the pork tenderloin during the last ½ hour of smoking. Pork is ready when the internal temperature reaches 165°F. Note: The tenderloin's internal temperature will continue to increase by 5-10 degrees after you pull it off the grill.

How To: Easy Dry Rub Grilled Pork Tenderloin

Ingredients:

- 1.5 Lbs Pork Tenderloin (Trimmed and Pat Dry)
- 1 Tbsp Brown Sugar
- 1 Tbsp Garlic Powder
- 1 Tbsp Chili Powder
- 1 Tbsp Salt
- 1 Tbsp Black Pepper
- 1 Tsp Smoked Paprika
- 1 Tsp Red Chili Flake

Directions:

1. Preheat Char-Griller Grill to high heat. For an easy weeknight dinner, I use the gas side of my Texas Trio for quick cooking, but of course, charcoal flavor would only add to this recipe! While grill is heating, mix spices together, sprinkle heavily over the meat, and rub well. Allow the meat to sit at room temperature for about 20 minutes, letting the spices marry. When grill has reached high heat, add pork loin and close lid. In 5 minutes, rotate meat clockwise to make diamond marks, and allow to cook another 5 minutes with the lid closed. After 10 minutes on one side has passed, flip your pork, and repeat- 5 minutes in one position with the lid closed, and rotate again, 5 minutes with the lid closed. I like to pull my pork off the grill at 145 degrees. While it rests, it will come up about 5-8 more degrees, allowing the meat to stay perfectly moist. Remove meat from the grill, cover loosely with foil, and let rest for 15 minutes before slicing. Serve with your favorite grilled vegetable or a large tossed salad. Enjoy!

OTHER FAVORITE RECIPES

Flavor Pro Bacon Wrapped Jalapeño Poppers

Cooking Time: 20 To 25 Min

Ingredients:

- 10 Jalapeno Peppers
- 1 (8 oz) Package of Cream Cheese, Softened
- 1 Package of Shredded Cheddar Cheese
- 20 Slices of Thin Cut Bacon
- 1/2 tsp Chipotle Powder
- 1/2 tsp Garlic Powder
- Salt and Pepper to Taste

Directions:

1. Halve the jalapeños and clean out all the seeds.
2. Mix together the cream cheese, 1 cup of cheddar cheese, chipotle powder, garlic powder, salt and pepper.
3. Fill the pepper halves with cream cheese mixture.
4. Wrap the peppers in strips of bacon.
5. Set up the Flavor Pro for direct cooking
6. Add 20 to 30 charcoal briquettes to the flavor drawer
7. Ignite charcoal with gas burners set to medium high
8. Once charcoal is lit, turn off gas burners and allow to fully ash over.
9. At this point, you can add a handful of soaked wood chips if desired.
10. Place wrapped jalapeños on grill for 20 to 25 minutes or until bacon is crispy.
11. Remove from grill and serve.

Grillinguy's Best Veggie Burger

Cooking Time: 10 Min

Ingredients:

- 1 Tbsp Olive Oil
- 1/2 Of a Sweet Onion (Minced)
- 3 Garlic Cloves (Minced)
- 1 Cup Cooked Quinoa
- 2 Cups Walnuts
- 1 15 Oz Can Of Pinto Beans
- 1/4 Cup Italian Seasoning
- 1/3 Cup Breadcrumbs
- 1 Tbsp Soy Sauce
- 1 Tsp Chili Powder
- 1 Tsp Cumin
- 1 Tsp Salt

Directions:

1. In a skillet over medium heat, add olive oil. Add onion and sauté until soften Add garlic and sauté for 30 seconds Set aside in a large bowl In food processor, add walnuts and pulse until crumb-like consistency. Add to bowl with onions Mash pintos and add to bowl Add in quinoa, soy sauce, Italian seasoning, chili powder, cumin, bread crumbs and salt Form into patties and place on baking sheet lined with parchment paper and refrigerate for an hour When ready to cook, preheat grill to medium high heat. Add patties and cook until brown on both sides Layer your bun with favorite toppings and enjoy

Smoked & Spiced Pumpkin Seeds

Ingredients:

- 3 - 4 Cups Fresh Pumpkin Seeds
- 3 Tbsp Salt
- 12 oz Water
- Olive Oil

Directions:

1. Cut open the top of the pumpkin and remove all the fibrous strands (pumpkin brains) inside and set aside.
2. Begin to separate the seeds from the fibrous strands and discard all the fibrous strands and set seeds aside.
3. Rinse pumpkin seeds in running water in the sink and continue to discard any remaining fibrous strands.
4. In a bowl add 12 oz. water with 2 tsp salt and mix thoroughly.
5. Add the pumpkin seeds to the mixture and place in the refrigerator for 2-24 hours.
6. Preheat your Char-griller Smokin' Champ 1624 to 300°
7. Tip: Ignite charcoal first, then add your favorite smoking wood.
8. Add small amount of water to your Char-griller drip pan for moisture.
9. Remove pumpkin seeds from the refrigerator and strain water
10. Add a drip of olive oil to the seeds and stir.
11. Add 1 tsp salt with a few sprinkles of Tajin to taste and stir thoroughly.
12. Then place the seeds on a large aluminum tray with a sheet of parchment paper and spread them evenly
13. Then place the large tray with the seeds to the smoker.
14. Maintain your fire at 300°
15. Rotate the tray periodically.
16. Remove seeds from the smoker after 1 hour of smoking or until golden brown.
17. Add a few fresh sprinkles of Tajin and enjoy!

Smoked Chex Mix

Cooking Time: 1-1½ Hrs

Ingredients:

- 3 C. corn Chex cereal
- 3 C. rice Chex cereal
- 3 C. wheat Chex cereal
- 1 C. mixed nuts
- 1 C. mini pretzels
- 6 Tbsp. unsalted butter
- 2 Tbsp. Worcestershire sauce
- 1½ Tsp. seasoned salt
- ¾ Tsp. garlic powder
- ½ Tsp. onion powder
- 1 Tsp. cayenne pepper, optional

Directions:

1. Pre-heat grill to 250°F. Melt butter in a small pan and mix in Worcestershire sauce, seasoned salt, onion powder, garlic powder, and cayenne pepper, if using. 2. Place Chex cereal, mini pretzels and mixed nuts in a large roasting pan. Add melted butter mixture and stir to evenly coat. 3. Place pan on the grill and smoke at 250°F for 1-1 ½ hours, and stir every 15-20 minutes. 4. Remove pan from grill and spread smoked Chex mix on paper towel-lined plate to cool.

2. Store in an airtight container or storage bag. Enjoy!

Smoked Bacon Wrapped Water Chestnuts

Ingredients:

- 1 Lb Bacon
- 2 (8 oz) cans of Water Chestnuts
- 1 Cup Packed Brown Sugar
- 2 Cups Ketchup
- 2 Tbsp Worcestershire Sauce
- 2 Tbsp Dijon Mustard
- Toothpicks

Directions:

1. Prepare AKORN or charcoal grill for 375°F
2. Add mild smoking wood like maple or apple for smoke flavor
3. Cut bacon slices in half. Wrap one slice of bacon around each chestnut. (For sliced water chestnuts, stack them three high, then wrap) Secure the wrap with a toothpick. Arrange the wraps in a foil pan or baking dish
4. In a medium-sized mixing bowl, combine ketchup, brown sugar, Worcestershire sauce, and mustard and stir well. Set aside.
5. Bake the wraps with no sauce for 10 to 15 minutes
6. Remove from wraps and drain out 75% of the grease. Keep the rest in pan.
7. Pour the sauce over the wraps. Be sure all wraps are coated well.
8. Bake/Smoke for 30-35 minutes.
9. Serve immediately and enjoy!

Cheesy, Bacon Bbq Meatloaf

Ingredients:

- 2 Lbs 80/20 Ground Beef
- 1 Lb Ground Pork
- 1/2 Yellow Onion (Diced)
- 1/2 Cup Bacon (Cut Up)
- 2 Cups Break Crumbs
- 3 Fresh Eggs
- Choice of BBQ Rub
- Choice of BBQ Sauce
- Package Of Mozzarella Cheese
- 1/2 Cup Brown Sugar

Directions:

1. Cook up the bacon and onions on your griddle or in a frying pan Let cool 30 mins Mix the ingredients in a large bowl Pack the mixture into two regular sized loaf pans Sit in fridge for at least 1hr to harden up Cook on your smoker at 275-200 degrees (F) until 140(F) internal temp Glaze with your favorite BBQ sauce Continue to cook until internal temp is 160(F) Let rest 10-15 minutes Slice and enjoy!

Perfect Ribeye Steaks On The Akorn

Cooking Time: 30 Min

Ingredients:

- Ribeye Steaks From Butcher Or Local Market
- 5-6 Medium Potatoes
- Couple Handfuls Of Green Beans
- Butter
- Olive Oil
- Salt/Pepper to Taste

Directions:

1. Set Akorn/Kamado to about 400 degrees F Take Steaks out of fridge, pat down with paper towels, drizzle and wipe down with small amount of olive oil and season with your favorite spices! Salt and Pepper are fine here. I like to leave the steaks out of fridge at this point on the counter, but you may put back in fridge if you like. Slice/chop up potatoes into 1" cubes, place in aluminum foil packet with butter and your favorite spices (again, salt/pepper will taste great!) Place green beans in aluminum foil packet with butter and favorite spices Once grill is up to temp, place potatoes and green beans directly on the grates. After 20 minutes, flip potatoes and green beans 15-20 minutes later remove potatoes and green beans Let grill raise temp until about 450-500 F Place steaks directly on grill and let cook for 2 minutes Twist steaks 90 degrees and let sit for 2 minutes (creates the crosshatch) Flip steaks and let cook for 2 minutes Twist steaks and let cook for 2 minutes You should now be at rare / medium rare - continue to cook until you reach the desired temperature your family likes. Enjoy!

Hickory Smoked Deviled Eggs

Cooking Time: 45 Min

Ingredients:

- Eggs - 6
- Soaked Hickory Wood Chips
- Mayonnaise - 1/4 Cup
- Yellow Mustard - 1 Tablespoon
- Hot Sauce - 2 Teaspoons
- Apple Cider Vinegar - 2 Teaspoons
- Sea Salt and Pepper to Taste

Directions:

1. Hard boil six eggs. My fool proof method: put the eggs in a pot of water over high heat, bring to a boil, turn off and cover, let sit for exactly ten minutes, then drop eggs in an ice water bath.

2. Peel the eggs and smoke using water soaked hickory wood chips for 30 minutes, rotating half way through, or until you reach the desired amount of color.

3. Slice the eggs in half, remove the yolks, and thoroughly mix them with the ingredients

4. Pipe the yolk mixture into the egg whites and top with paprika, crumbled bacon, and chopped green onions.

Smoked Roasted Vegetables

Cooking Time: 15 Min

Ingredients:

- ➢ 1 medium onion
- ➢ 1 zucchini
- ➢ 1 small green bell pepper
- ➢ 1 small red bell pepper
- ➢ 1 small yellow bell pepper
- ➢ Vegetable oil, for brushing
- ➢ Salt and pepper, to taste

Directions:

1. Pre-heat grill to 400°F. Rinse all produce and pat dry with paper towel. 2. Slice bell peppers in half and remove stem, core and seeds. Remove outer layers of onion and slice in half. Slice zucchini in half and remove ends. 3. Place vegetables on grill, equally spaced apart and grill for 10-12 minutes, turning occasionally, until vegetables are tender and grill marks develop. Skins of bell peppers should be lightly charred. 4. Lightly brush vegetables with olive oil. Sprinkle with salt and pepper or your favorite seasoning.

2. Slice vegetables into 1" strips when cooled enough to handle and serve. Enjoy!

Bacon Wrapped Apples With Sweet Bourbon Glaze

Cooking Time: 25 Min

Ingredients:

➢ Bacon - 1 lb

➢ 4 Gala Apples

➢ 1/4 Cup Granulated Sugar

➢ Cinnamon - 1 Tbs

➢ 1/2 Cup Powdered Sugar

➢ 1 Stick Butter, Melted

➢ Bourbon Whiskey - 1 Tbsp

Directions:

1. Prepare Char-Griller AKORN for indirect heat at 350°

2. Optional: Add applewood for a kiss of smoke flavor

3. Slice off both ends of each apple. Using a smaller, flexible knife or apple corer remove cores and seeds

4. Slice de-cored apples horizontally to make O-shapes. Be sure to cut each slice's width as evenly as possible

5. Cut bacon slices into half. Use a half slice of bacon for each apple-O. Start by weaving one end of the bacon through the top of the hole and under the bottom, bringing it back over the top of the apple. Then bring the other end over to hold it in place, continuing to weave bacon around the remaining parts of the apple using the same method

6. Tip: Thin sliced bacon works better with this recipe because it is easier to maneuver and stretch around the apple

7. In a bowl, combine cinnamon and sugar. Sprinkle generously onto each side of the apple

8. Place apples on a pizza stone, wire rack, or baking pan. Put inside the Akorn and bake for 25 min at 350° or until apples are soft but still have bite and bacon has browned and caramelized

9. Making glaze: While apples bake, melt butter in saucepan over low heat. Once melted, slowly sift and stir in powdered sugar. Simmer until combined and add bourbon. Simmer a bit longer until alcohol taste has cooked out

10. Let cool for 1-2 min then drizzle over apples. Top with more cinnamon and sugar if desired. Enjoy!

Smokin' Whole Bone-in Ham

Cooking Time: 7 Hrs

Ingredients:

- Fresh Whole Bone-In Ham: 18 pounds
- Olive Oil: Small Coat, Used for a Binder
- Char-Griller Grills Creole and Sweet & Spicy Seasonings: to taste
- Sazon Seasoning: to taste
- Char-Griller Grills Smokin' Champ 1733
- Lump Charcoal & Mesquite Smoking Wood
- Char-Griller Grills Drip Pan
- Char-Griller Grills Charcoal Chimney
- Char-Griller Grills Remote Thermometer
- Favorite Glaze: I used a homemade Spicy Strawberry & Raspberry glaze

Directions:

1. Prepping Directions
2. Using a sharp knife, score the fat on top of the ham on a diagonal into squares. This helps the seasonings penetrate the meat and allows extra smoke into the meat. Coat all sides with olive oil. Season all sides with Char-Griller Grills Creole, Sweet & Spicy and Sazon Seasonings to taste It's now ready for the smoker!
3. Smoking Directions
4. Clean out the Char-Griller Smokin' Champ 1733 smoker and insert the Char-Griller Grills Drip Pan filled with water to the top into the main cooking area under the grill grates in the ash pan area. Using the Char-Griller Grills Charcoal Chimney fire up a full chimney of lump charcoal to 250°-300°. Release the lump charcoal on top a mesquite smoking log. Allow the smoker to thoroughly warm up, about 20 minutes. Place the ham in the smoker over the drip pan. Check in on the ham and side firebox every 60 minutes. Rotate the ham for an even smoke and also add lump charcoal/Smoking wood as needed. Insert the Char-Griller Grills Remote Thermometer to monitor the internal temperature. Smoke ham to internal temperature 135° then glaze all sides of the ham with your favorite glaze. Smoke the glazed ham to internal temperature 140°. Remove the ham from the smoker and allow it to rest for 30 minutes. Slice and enjoy!

Gravity 980 Quick N' Fast Grilled Vegetables

Cooking Time: 5 Min

Ingredients:

- 1 Large Zucchini (Sliced)
- 1 Large Summer Squash (Sliced)
- 1 Red Bed Pepper (Sliced)
- 3 Large Portobello Mushrooms (Sliced)
- 1 Red Onion (Sliced)
- Kosher Salt
- Black Pepper
- 1 Tbsp of Garlic Powder
- 1 Tsp of Paprika
- 1 Tbsp of Italian Seasoning (or your choice of herbs)
- 1/2 Cup of Extra Virgin Olive Oil

Directions:

1. Remove the fire shutter from the Gravity 980. Load the hopper and set the temperature to 400°F. In a large bowl, combine all veggies with olive oil and seasonings. Place a grill wok on the grates and close the grill, allowing it to preheat for 2-3 minutes before adding vegetable mixture. Using a silicone spatula, open the grill and stir vegetables around in the wok, repeating the process until vegetables reach desired doneness. Serve hot or warm. Enjoy!

Candied Bacon Recipe

Cooking Time: 35 Min

Ingredients:

- ➢ 9 Slices of Bacon
- ➢ Brown Sugar - 1/3 Cup
- ➢ Cinnamon - 1/4 tsp
- ➢ Black Pepper - 1/4 tsp

Directions:

1. Heat grill to 350 indirect heat. Combine brown sugar, cinnamon, and pepper in a small bowl. Dip each piece of bacon, front and back, in sugar mixture. Place bacon strips on a greased wire rack. Sprinkle remaining sugar over bacon. Place rack on the grill grates and cook bacon for 30-35 minutes until crispy. Remove from grill and allow to cool. Chop the bacon into small pieces. Place a small handful of bacon aside for topping. Make the bourbon glaze.

Smoked Irish-style Lamb And Potatoes

Cooking Time: 3 Hrs

Ingredients:

- 4-5 lb. boneless leg of lamb
- 3 Tbsp. fresh rosemary
- 6 cloves garlic, minced and divided into 3rds
- 2 Tbsp. black pepper
- 3 Tbsp. Kosher salt
- 3 Tbsp. olive oil
- 15 medium potatoes, quartered
- 1 C. diced onion
- 1 bell pepper, seeded and diced
- Kitchen twine for tying
- Aluminum baking pan

Directions:

1. Rinse lamb and pat dry with paper towel.
2. Combine rosemary, 2/3 of minced garlic (4 cloves), 2 Tbsp. salt, pepper and olive oil into a small bowl and mix well.
3. Rub mixture all over lamb and tie securely in multiple spots with kitchen twine. Snip off any excess twine.
4. Combine potatoes, onion, pepper, remaining 1/3 of minced garlic (2 cloves), and 1 Tbsp. salt into sturdy pan. Mix well and set aside.
5. Add smokin' stone/heat deflector, place lamb on warming rack, and smoke at 250°F for 1 hour.
6. Place pan with potato mixture on grate under lamb (to catch drippings) and smoke for another 2 hours. Lamb is done when internal temperature reaches 140°F, for medium-rare.
7. Remove lamb from the grill, allow to rest for 20 minutes before slicing in 1"-1½" increments.
8. Cut and remove kitchen twine before serving.

Raptor Claws

Cooking Time: 2 Hrs

Ingredients:

- ➢ 4 jalapeño peppers
- ➢ 1 lb. ground sausage, divided into 4 equal parts
- ➢ Jalapeño cream cheese
- ➢ Original All-Purpose BBQ rub, to taste
- ➢ Favorite BBQ sauce

Directions:

1. Pre-heat grill to 250°F. Rinse jalapeños and pat dry with paper towel. 2. Cut the top off each jalapeño and remove the core and seeds. 3. Stuff with cream cheese. 4. Wrap ¼ lb. of sausage around each jalapeño, starting from the open end and leaving the tip of the jalapeño uncovered. 5. Season sausage with your favorite rub, or use Original All-Purpose BBQ rub, to taste. 6. Place on the grill at 250°F to smoke for 1 hour before turning. 7. Smoke for another 30-45 minutes. 8. Baste with your favorite BBQ sauce and smoke for an additional 15 minutes.

2. Remove from grill, allow to cool and serve.

Printed by Libri Plureos GmbH in Hamburg,
Germany